Listening

for a

Lifetime

Readers are encouraged to go to www.MissionPointPress.com to contact the author, or to contact the publisher about how to buy this book in bulk at a discounted rate.

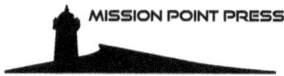
MISSION POINT PRESS

Published by Mission Point Press
2554 Chandler Road
Traverse City, Michigan 49696
(231) 421-9513
www.MissionPointPress.com

Hardcover: 978-1-961302-92-1
Softcover: 978-1-961302-93-8

Library of Congress Control Number: 2024915511

Printed in the United States of America

Listening
for a
Lifetime

The Artful Science
of Psychotherapy

David I Joseph MD

MISSION POINT PRESS

For Alice, with love

"ONLY CONNECT THE PROSE AND THE PASSION
AND BOTH SHALL BE EXALTED"
—E. M. FORSTER

TABLE OF CONTENTS

PREFACE

I hope that perusing the preface and table of contents will pique your interest. Each listing is a phrase I created during my professional career. Taken together they provide a framework for understanding how, in my professional practice, I think and work. My perspective, like the sayings themselves, is quite personal, reflecting my conviction that psychoanalysis and psychoanalytic psychotherapy are both deeply personal and solidly professional. The psychoanalytic relationship, like any meaningful relationship, develops over time, and, while theories shape the conversation between patient and therapist, their relationship is built from innumerable, intimate moment-to-moment interactions.

Listening for a Lifetime is, in important ways, a memoir, a "shaped narrative around a single theme" (McDonnell 1998, 104). To a significant degree, all psychoanalytic writing, especially clinical writing, shares much with memoir. As Gornick (1998) has emphasized, creating a memoir "turns out to be as dramatic an exercise as the attempt at psychoanalysis: fraught with anxiety, a struggle to focus, difficult to achieve distance, and painfully hard to identify the 'real story.'" I suspect that Gornick is giving voice to the experience of a patient immersed in a deeply meaningful personal psychoanalysis, but her words evocatively capture the experience of a practicing psychoanalyst as well as a patient.

FROM TEACHER TO AUTHOR

The pleasure at being admired is intense, volatile, and evaporates quickly. The pain of self-loathing is intense, painful, and enduring.

The person who acts violently feels they have been violated.

If you think of the mind as a harp, over the course of your career your patients will pluck every string in the harp of your mind, including some that you had no idea were there.

Don't let insurance companies or lawyers tell you how to practice your profession.

Don't assume anything. If you're right, you're lucky and you will likely be wrong.

Every adopted child has to come to terms with the fact that they were given away by their mother.

These are some of the many maxims I created over the course of my career that I may have shared with Fred Pisoni, Kit Maclean, and Martha Dupecher. I say "may," because I have no idea which maxim led each of them to say they found my way of thinking about and expressing psychoanalytic concepts to be clear, succinct, and helpful. Each also urged me to write a book, an undertaking I had never considered. Fred and Kit were studying to become psycho-analysts, and I was one of their clinical supervisors. Martha was a fellow faculty member at the Washington-Baltimore Center for Psychoanalysis. We had taught a course on psychoanalytic writing and her encouragement tipped the scale. I took the bit between my teeth and was off to the races.

For several years during supervisory hours and after clinical sessions, if something I said seemed especially noteworthy and, in a condensed way, reflected an important aspect of how I think and work, I would jot it down on a 3x5 card. Surprisingly, in six months the list had burgeoned to well over a hundred entries, and the number continued to grow steadily.

I believe that the essential aspects of psychoanalytic thought and practice can be expressed clearly and concisely and can be readily understood and applied. That conviction nurtured the creation of these sayings, albeit without my focusing on the process at all.

Without any forethought, I stored the list of maxims in my computer under the heading "Joseph's aphorisms," unaware that the word, "aphorism," was coined by Hippocrates in *The Aphorisms of Hippocrates*, a collection of propositions regarding the practice of medicine and the art of healing. Over time, the definition evolved and now refers to "any principle or precept expressed in a few words; a short, pithy sentence containing a truth of general import; a maxim" (Oxford English Dictionary).

It is serendipitous indeed that the origins of "aphorism" lie in the writings of Hippocrates, one of the most influential physicians in the history of medicine. Each item I added to my burgeoning list was a concise proposition of something I consider central to a psychoanalytic understanding of the mind, including its motivations, emotions, thoughts, dreams, fantasies, and actions. Each aphorism also conveys an important aspect of the way I practice the professions of medicine, psychiatry, and psychoanalysis, be it in the role of clinician, supervisor, teacher, or administrator. These maxims most certainly are not propositions of essential psychoanalytic truths, but they are central to who I am, how I think, and how I work. Regardless of the patient I am treating, or whether I am a teacher, supervisor, or administrator, I am always a psychoanalyst. Although it may not be apparent, my psychoanalytic mind remains very much at the center of my person.

Defining and describing a "psychoanalytic process" is both a creative and a scientific endeavor, but efforts to formulate sharp distinctions between psychoanalytic psychotherapy and psychoanalysis are often infused with undercurrents of superiority and status. Rarely, in my experience, have such discussions increased understanding or improved patient care and, at times, an analyst's wish to avoid introducing "psychotherapeutic" methods into the psychoanalysis proves harmful to the patient.

Throughout this book I will use psychotherapy and psychoanalysis interchangeably. In every respect, I bring a deep, broad psychoanalytic perspective to my work, and I carry a powerful conviction that therapists who have immersed themselves in a meaningful, intensive, and personal psychoanalytic psychotherapy will be better able to practice their profession. Those who eschew or mock the importance of this aspect of a psychotherapist's education are denying the importance of their unconscious minds and the impact of unconscious psychic forces on how they listen, what they hear, and the ways in which they work. I believe that the ideas conveyed in these aphorisms are applicable to cognitive behavioral therapy, crisis intervention, family and group psychotherapy—indeed all psychotherapies—and hope that they will be useful to other health care providers as well.

As a resident in psychiatry at Yale, I heard of Elvin Semrad, MD, a legendary psychiatrist at the Massachusetts Mental Health Center whose well chosen words conveyed the wisdom he had accumulated over the years. After his death, two residents who had studied with him incorporated his memorable thoughts and clinical observations into a book, *Semrad, the Heart of a Therapist* (Rako, S. and Mazer, H. 1980). As I was gathering my aphorisms, I remembered learning about this book, but resisted reading it until I was well into a second draft of my book. And, when I had finished it, I wished he had expanded upon the brief sayings that his students recalled. I am certain that Elvin Semrad was very much in the back of my mind as I created the aphorisms that organize this book.

While writing this book, I frequently wandered into exploring topics that were very personal to me and my ways of thinking and working. My initial impulse to eliminate the more personal aspects of my self and my work was quickly outweighed by the conviction that, without a meaningful exploration about who I am as a person practicing psychoanalysis, any discussion of my ideas about psychoanalytic theory and practice would be incomplete and quietly misleading.

While surgeons must set their personal selves aside when they enter the operating room, psychoanalysts and psychotherapists place their person at the center of their work. The interplay between the analyst's technical skills and their person—its rhythms, tones, nuances, and harmonies—form the foundation of psychotherapy. A Mozart string quartet will be immediately recognizable, regardless of the performers. Similarities between one psychoanalytic experi-ence and another are rather few.

At the conclusion of this endeavor, I hope you will have mean-ingfully come to know me, someone who has had the remarkable privilege of being a physician, a psychiatrist, and a psychoanalyst for over 50 years. Through an exploration of these aphorisms, I will invite you into the consulting room of my mind.

PSYCHOANALYSIS
IS AN ARTFUL SCIENCE

The title for this book reflects my conviction that listening occupies the very center of the psychotherapeutic relationship. Hearing is an involuntary, neurophysiolgic event, an event of the brain. Listening is a voluntary, psychological act, an act of the mind. We listen because we want to understand the sounds and communications we are hearing.

Barthes (1991) has evocatively explored the experience of listening, emphasizing that it involves alertness, the awareness of cues from the environment, deciphering the identification of patterns embodied in the sounds one perceives, and understanding the impact of what one says upon the other person. Barthes stresses that psychoanalytic listening depends on the ability of the psychoanalytic listener to avoid judgment, thereby freeing them to think more fluidly and develop a better understanding of the patient's unconscious communications. The complexity and profound implications of meaningful listening comprise the very essence of the psychoanalytic experience.

Psychoanalytic listening, free association, and the process of writing share a subtle but meaningfully altered state of consciousness. Psychoanalytic remembering also involves an imperceptible change in consciousness, enabling the ability to recall information from sessions long past. Patients often wonder how I remember so much about them and how rarely I confuse their lives with those of other patients. This ability does not reflect an extraordinary memory, at least not the kind necessary to know the 206 bones in the human body or to perform another task of recall that might benefit from some mnemonic technique. Instead, the explanation lies in the very nature of psychoanalytic listening.

Ironically, psychoanalytic forgetting is an unsettling cousin of psychoanalytic remembering. The very elements of psychoanalytic listening that facilitate making emotional connections and recalling aspects of the patient's history also make it very difficult to remember much, if anything, of my previous conversation with the patient, even if we met 24 hours earlier. Sometimes, a specific emotionally charged or traumatic experience fails to become a topic for exploration and seems to have been eliminated from my memory as well as from the patient's. I understand such "forgetting" as a powerful indication of the patient's desire that neither of us remember what they desperately would like to erase.

Sometimes I take notes after a session for future use in teaching or writing, but I never review my notes prior to meeting with a patient. Such preparation would shape a very different experience and conversation, one that privileges historical rather than psychoanalytic continuity. Even if desirable, "Picking up where we left off" is impossible. The patient and I have spent time apart, and I attempt to assume nothing about where the patient is likely to begin. I trust that, between us, we will remember what we need to remember. The desire to "pick up where we left off" also reflects the wish that patient and analyst, whose separate and autonomous lives intersect in the odd, intimate experience we call psychoanalysis, were able to have a relationship outside the psychoanalytic context.

I use "psychoanalysis" to refer to the clinical treatment of patients employing psychoanalytic principles and techniques, but it would be more accurate to say, "applied psychoanalysis." Psychoanalysis is a theory of mind and behavior which is rooted in the understanding that Freud and other analysts developed from their experience with patients. The psychoanalytic understanding of mind has been greatly enriched and deepened by over 100 years of clinical experience and by extensive psychological and neurophysiological research.

In addition to furthering clinical treatment, this perspective has been used to deepen our understanding of historical figures, child development, film, and other subjects. In recent years, clinical psychoanalysis has been devalued and sometimes denigrated by departments of psychiatry and psychology (McWilliams, N. and Slochower, J., personal communication, 2023) in the United States.

ORIENTING PRINCIPLES

The aphorisms in this section explore concepts that are central to my clinical work, regardless of the patient or the setting. Taken together, they provide a broad, solid foundation for initiating a relationship with the patient with the goal of determining a diagnosis and developing a plan of treatment. If the patient feels understood and respected, and can see a way forward that will relieve their distress, the experience will be "therapeutic."

<><><><><><><><><><><><><><><><><><><><><><><><><><><>

I PROVIDE CARE TO PATIENTS, NOT CLIENTS.

Anyone who comes to me for assistance becomes my patient. As a physician and psychiatrist, the culture of my educational institutions always referred to those under our care as patients, Not long after completing my psychiatric residency in 1971, other mental health care providers expressed unhappiness with applying this name to those who sought their help, believing that "patient" implied that the person in their care was "sick," while the caregiver was "healthy." They thought that this implicit distinction introduced a hurtful, hierarchical dynamic into the therapeutic relationship, a situation that was rectified by considering those in their care to be "clients."

I continued to consider individuals in my care to be my "patients." To do otherwise seemed awkward and demeaning to them, to our relationship, and to my profession. My steadfast commitment to my "patients" was reinforced by discovering that our current usage of "patient" evolved from the Latin word *patiens*, or "one who suffers." All individuals who seek our care do so in hopes that we can alleviate their suffering. Since the alleviation of psychological suffering is often gradual and infused with new pain—the product of deepening self-discovery—being a patient requires considerable patience. Providing care to a person in pain requires considerable patience as well.

"Therapy" derives from the Latin noun *therapia*, which is rooted in the Greek word for curing or healing. Linguistically, patients seek our assistance to heal their suffering. "Psyche," a French word, derives from the Greek term for soul or spirit. And "soul," whose linguistic ancestor is the middle English word *soule*, refers to the "spiritual or immaterial part of a person" (OED). Our patients enter into a relationship with us hoping that we can heal the suffering of their souls, that we can administer care to the "incorporeal essence" of their person. Psychotherapy, the mutual effort of patient and therapist to heal the soul of the patient, often develops an ineffable "spiritual" dimension.

For myself, being a psychoanalyst reflects deep respect for the power of unconscious thought, emotion, and motivation. It also conveys an understanding that genetic inheritance, constitutional nature, experiences in childhood and throughout life, and sociocultural forces shape the person we become. The adult brain and mind are surprisingly plastic and, in the environment of the right relationship, new learning and meaningful transformation can occur, regardless of the patient's age or the severity of their psychiatric disorder. Being a psychoanalyst also reflects the belief that a patient's private sense of themselves, their relationships, and the pursuit of their personal aspirations will be significantly furthered by a greater awareness about their previously unconscious mind.

Not attaching any adjective such as Freudian, Kleinian, Kohution, or interpersonal (I am always tempted to say "good") to "psychoanalyst" conveys my conviction that all the schools of psychoanalytic thought accurately and meaningfully conceptualize a central aspect of being human (Pine 2011). To privilege one theoretical perspective allows for consistency, but I believe a deeper understanding grows from determining which perspective is most "alive" in the clinical moment. It is as though I am on an automobile trip, listening to the radio, and needing to carefully scan the frequencies to determine which signal is strongest. Patients need us to discover and then attune ourselves to the station whose signal is strongest at a given clinical moment.

Over time, they will broadcast in many different wavelengths, and we can never assume which will be most accessible on a given day. Listening to patients resembles listening to a string quartet in which the four individual parts that meld to form a whole can also be listened to individually. A clinician's attempt to be "attuned" requires listening with a musical frame of mind as well as thinking with an analytic mind.

◇◇◇

ANYONE WHO KNOCKS ON YOUR DOOR IS SUFFERING.

Discovering the linguistic relationship between "patient" and "suffering" reinforced a conviction that has long been at the foundation of my clinical work, one that I have returned to repeatedly over my entire career. This aphorism holds that "Anyone who knocks on your door is suffering." This unshakable belief has proven invaluable, rescuing me from sinking into confusion and therapeutic despair with patients who are unaware of any psychological pain. Such patients cannot define what they seek from treatment, yet continue to see me regularly, pay my full fee promptly, express no wish to change anything about themselves, and never consider ending treatment. Often urged to seek treatment by a significant other, a superior at work, another physician, or, in extreme situations, ordered by the courts, these patients comply and find it meaningful simply to speak with me on a regular basis, never experiencing themselves as "being in therapy."

As this type of clinical relationship evolves, I often begin to feel useless and unworthy of the fee the patient so willingly pays. Over time, a combination of thinking that I am tangential to the patient's life and inadequate as a therapist grows and nurtures the enduring thought that I should refer the patient to someone else who might be better able to help them. In such situations, I wonder whether the patient has evoked in me the very sense of inadequacy and failure that has been rendered unconscious by them.

While patients seem determined to experience themselves as living an enjoyable and satisfying life and finds our time together valuable, the conviction that only someone in pain would continue to meet with me has sustained me. This conviction also challenges my unsettling doubt that I am not helping them at all. Sometimes, referral to another psychotherapist is the better choice, but that determination is best held in abeyance for a considerable time while one tries to understand and address the patient's dread of experiencing their own, unconscious suffering.

Every psychotherapist needs to have a modest but meaningful understanding of how their mind works; that is why their own personal, intensive psychoanalytic or other insight-oriented psychotherapy is essential. I believe that it is equally important that our patients come to learn how we experience our relationship with them, what has led to our understanding aspects of themselves of which they had been unaware, and what informs our interventions. Our work as teachers and supervisors depends on an ability to convey how we think. It is equally important that we provide such understanding to our patients.

Many patients have grown up believing that their parents and other important people are threatened by and tenaciously avoid being known. While this is most dramatically exemplified by "family secrets," more subtle exhortations to blunt one's curiosity are quietly conveyed and absorbed in childhood. Children often mistakenly attribute emotions and thoughts that originate from their own minds as coming from their parents' anxieties. However, parental opacity will reinforce whatever inhibitions children may have about knowing both themselves and others.

I have wondered whether adults who have difficulty "mentalizing"

(Allen, Fonagy and Bateman 2008) may have grown up in families in which the parents did not want to be known and hid their minds behind an opaque yet seemingly engaged and open persona. I think that it always furthers the therapy for a patient to know how I have arrived at a given hypothesis. (I consider all interpretations to be hypotheses.) When a patient inquires, "What led you to say that?" I believe it is helpful, after some exploration of what prompted the question, to provide an answer, even if the answer is "I just had a hunch"—an uncommon response but one that is not offered defensively. When and in what ways a particular psychotherapy is furthered by self-disclosure will be explored later, but implacable non-disclosure is undesirable, and is especially hurtful to patients whose parents resolutely avoided being known. Hiding one's self differs markedly from choosing, in a given clinical moment, to keep one's self private.

Before going further, a confession seems essential. Often I do not recall where I learned something, and I have always envied colleagues who can cite articles that demonstrated a specific point. In what follows, I will acknowledge a source when I am sure of it, although I am certain that I will fail to give credit to many individuals whose wisdom I absorbed; to them I can only offer a heartfelt apology.

I have grouped my aphorisms into categories covering many aspects of the practice of psychoanalysis, beginning with the initial patient contact and concluding with thoughts about retirement, a process that I was experiencing during the period in which I was writing this book. When you arrive at the book's conclusion, I hope you will develop a meaningful sense of how I inhabit the role of the psychotherapist.

David I Joseph MD

YOU WILL BE LIKED AND RESPECTED FOR DOING A GOOD JOB, NOT FOR BEING A "GOOD GUY."

I have no idea how long ago this saying came to me, although I am certain it reflects the influence of my father, who successfully ran a family business in which the personal and the commercial were inextricably interwoven. Early in my life, I developed innumerable subtle, creative ways to avoid disappointing others, yet remained oblivious to my own painful disappointments. So, for me to hold this conviction is profoundly ironic. When I encountered Roy Schafer's paper, "Disappointment and Disappointedness" (Schafer 1999), I appreciated more deeply the impact of disappointment in oneself and others and the corrosive impact of enduring disappointedness.

I initially thought this aphorism applied only to my professional self, both clinical and administrative. However, I incrementally came to realize how powerfully it shapes who I aspire to be in any role I inhabit. Understanding and applying the implications of this principle has made it easier to accept the responsibility of making decisions that will elicit pain from others, whether they be family, friends, patients, or colleagues. Equally important, knowing that I can accept and respect the consequences of my actions has allowed me to fashion more creative and often more helpful interventions in which the pain inflicted can be more readily metabolized and contribute to personal growth. Like any other principle, this one

16

can be subtly or bluntly misused and be invoked to rationalize unnecessarily harmful actions.

Tact is the ability to take a verbal or silent action at a time when it can be listened to, explored, and understood, even as the recipient experiences the pain and unhappiness it elicits. In the clinical setting, tact and timing make it possible for the patient to endure the discomfort that results from learning something that they have hidden from themselves. In all settings, the recipient of a tactful intervention will know that the clinician, supervisor, teacher, or manager believes they are being "cruel only to be kind," and will be able to reflect upon the new information in a manner that contributes to deeper understanding and meaningful change.

A young man whose father had died when he was young had found his treatment with me very helpful in reducing his anxiety in social situations and increasing his self-confidence in many aspects of his life. One spring day he invited me to join him at a Nationals baseball game, certain that I was an avid fan. After exploring what feelings had led to the invitation, I declined, explaining that, while going to the game together would be enjoyable, our work would be furthered more by my not joining him. I continued by saying that I respected his wish that we share this experience.

Hurt, angry, and near tears, he asked, "Why can't we be friends?" To my surprise, I found myself saying, with complete conviction and no defensiveness, "I can be the best friend possible by being the best analyst I can." Some years later, I would come to believe that a psychoanalytic "friendship" develops in the course of any meaningful psychotherapy—a topic I will explore in detail later.

This principle is also reflected in the challenges faced by patients as they try to fulfill the extraordinarily challenging, demanding job of being a patient in the psychotherapeutic relationship. When therapist and patient share a mutual understanding that the therapy will be most productive if the patient addresses what is most important to them, tries to give voice to whatever comes to mind without editing, or, in a brief, focused therapy, consistently and courageously explores a specific issue, the role and task of the patient is clearly defined. Their self-respect and the therapist's respect for them will be rooted in how well they fulfill their role. This is quite counter-intuitive, given that much of what patients need to confront and explore honestly with us are thoughts, feelings, and actions about which they are deeply ashamed and guilty, sometimes with good reason, and which are frequently directed toward us.

A patient who confesses that they have embezzled money from an older person whose account they manage or ashamedly recounts how, many years ago, they fondled the genitals of a young boy whom they were babysitting, elicits two very different responses from their therapist. Although they are very unlikely to give voice to it, the therapist holds a private conviction about the unethical behavior that inflicted harm on a vulnerable person. But the therapist also experiences deep respect for the way in which the patient's ruthless honesty has allowed them to confront and share their experience. In fulfilling their job well, the patient has furthered the work of the therapy and earned our deep respect, even as they simultaneously allow us to know an aspect of themselves that we judge negatively and disrespect. Similarly, while the patient knows that they have acted shamefully, they understand—often unconsciously—that they have earned the therapist's respect as well as their own self-respect by shouldering the hard work of therapy. I will explore the topic of respect in psychoanalysis more thoroughly in a subsequent section of this book.

In a meaningful therapy, every patient comes to understand that growth and transformation only take root when they have been willing to tolerate the pain of self-awareness. When applied to the patient, this maxim has its own twist. To succeed in the job of being a patient, the patient must, at times, be willing to be a "bad person" and put into verbal action the negative feelings they have about the therapist. To frame the dilemma differently, they are "doing a good job" by acting cruelly toward someone who cares about and is trying to provide care to them and whom they care about deeply. The therapist, fully committed to the conviction that no therapy can maximize its transformational potential if the patient does not convey whatever is on his mind at the moment, has to tolerate, as best they can, the unavoidable pain of the patient's hostility. I do not believe that it is in the patient's interest for therapists to allow themselves to be endlessly tortured, but, in my experience, a successful therapy often involves the therapist's ability to tolerate the patient's attacks, whether subtle or blunt.

〰〰〰〰〰〰〰〰〰〰〰〰〰〰〰〰〰〰〰〰〰〰〰〰〰〰〰

ALL CLINICIANS ARE PSYCHOTHERAPISTS.

In their relationship with patients, all professional health care workers are psychotherapists. They may be good psychotherapists, poor psychotherapists, indifferent psychotherapists, resentful psychotherapists, or completely unaware of being psychotherapists at all. They may derive satisfaction from this aspect of their profession or find it burdensome and deeply unsettling. They may understand and respect their patients' psychotherapeutic needs and gain satisfaction from addressing them. But they may also ignore them and sometimes react with discomfort, resentment, and quiet scorn. But while nurse's aides, neurosurgeons, and all other health care workers may be unaware of it, they are, in every interaction, with every patient, supportive psychotherapists.

Good health care is built upon a foundation of good, supportive psychotherapy. A consistent, caring, respectful relationship brings deeply meaningful comfort to frightened, confused, and sometimes "regressed" patients. To change the bed linens of a patient who has soiled himself without adding to the shame they already feel, to express concern about the level of the patient's pain, to console a grieving family, to sit quietly with a frightened child, or to listen non-judgmentally to whatever a patient wishes to share is central to being a good health care provider. Such a health care provider is a good and effective supportive psychotherapist.

Mental health professionals are much more likely to understand the centrality of the "supportive" aspect of psychotherapy, but the profession has developed roles which imply that supportive psychotherapy is not understood to be an essential component of their task or of their relationship with their patients. The impersonal title, "case manager," has transformed a person with a chronic, disabling disease into a "case," and a caregiver into a manager. Supportive psychotherapy may well play only a minimal part, if any part at all, in the case manager's understanding of their role. Ironically, if they perform the management responsibilities well, they may act harmfully, never aware of their importance to the patient, believing that they provide functions in which the personhood of the provider is not an important factor. They may perceive themselves more as managers of a store than a provider of care to a person in pain and need of assistance. While they may understand that a supportive relationship is present, they may well underestimate its centrality to the patient's sense of being cared for.

Mental health professionals in emergency rooms are under such stress and are required to make such immediate, difficult decisions that they may minimize the importance of psychotherapy to the patients they treat. Since the primary focus is on rapid assessment and disposition, and includes the awesome responsibility of deciding whether a patient can be safely treated outside the hospital, it's understandable that alleviating the patient's emotional suffering is not at the forefront of the clinician's mind.

I try to remember that every action I take with a patient, including scheduling appointments, greeting a patient in the waiting room, ending a session, negotiating a fee, or informing a patient of an absence, is a psychotherapeutic action. The action can either nurture or damage the patient and the therapy. Keeping this foremost in mind takes vigilance and effort; when it is ignored, patients are always hurt, whether or not patient or clinician allow themselves to be aware of it.

◇◇

A PSYCHOPHARMACOLOGIST IS NOT A CLINICIAN; A PHYSICIAN WHO PRESCRIBES MEDICATION IS A PHARMACOTHERAPIST, NOT A PSYCHOPHARMACOLOGIST.

A physician involved in laboratory research on the evaluation of medication in the treatment of a psychiatric patient is a psycho-pharmacologist. A psychiatrist or other physician who prescribes medication may well think of themselves as psychopharmacologists but, in so doing, they run the risk of not attending to the unique psychotherapy that is integral to the prescription of any medication. There is significant literature under the general heading, "Combining Psychotherapy and Medication," but the heading, itself, silently suggests that the prescription of medication does not involve a specialized kind of psychotherapy.

All patients who are taking medication and also engaged in psychoanalytic or any other kind of psychotherapy are involved in two psychotherapies: pharmacotherapy and some other kind of psychotherapy. Since all health care workers are psychothera-pists, any physician who prescribes medication is fulfilling two psychotherapeutic roles: a supportive psychotherapist and a phar-macotherapist. When a patient is participating in two psychothera-pies—pharmacotherapy and a different type of psychotherapy—they will have quite different relationships with the psychotherapist and the pharmacotherapist, even if both roles are fulfilled by the same clinician.

When discussing with a patient whether to add medication to the treatment regimen or to modify the current pharmacological regimen, a psychoanalytic psychotherapist inhabits a very different role. But even when the conversation is not concerned with medication, psychotherapists must always evaluate whether the current medication regimen is optimal, thereby assuming a pharmacotherapeutic role. They may not be consciously aware of doing so, but they are nonetheless. Likewise, the patient inhabits two very different roles: one devoted to increased understanding and personal growth, the other a role in which they choose to ingest a specific medication to alleviate specific symptoms and assess its impact.

In the clinical moment, neither patient nor psychiatrist is focused on the differences between and conflicts inherent in these two relationships. Although both may be unaware of or minimize the challenges of integrating these two roles, the structure of the treatment requires the integration of two roles and two relationships.

To avoid this problem, some psychoanalytic physicians will not become the patient's pharmacotherapist. They believe that the effectiveness of both the psychotherapy and the pharmacotherapy is increased by separating the two roles. Regardless of whether the pharmacotherapy and the psychotherapy are provided by the same or by different clinicians, complexities are inherent and have an important impact on the treatment.

Combining pharmacotherapy with psychotherapy creates a psychotherapist-medication split. When covering for a colleague who was taking an extended vacation, I was called by one of her patients who wanted to reduce the dosage of their medication.

The patient told me that they had been in twice-weekly psycho-analytic psychotherapy for several years and had been taking an antidepressant for nearly a year. When exploring their thinking about this desired change, the patient said they were concerned about becoming dependent on the medication, although they knew that it did not cause pharmacological addiction.

Quite clearly, they had focused their concern about "dependency" on the medication and were totally unaware that their fear of dependence stemmed from the important, meaningful relationship they had developed with their psychiatrist. Reducing the medication was their creative solution to concerns about dependency. By reducing the dosage of medication, they would decrease their anxiety concerning dependency without reducing the frequency of meeting with their analyst, thereby avoiding their unconscious fear regarding the importance of this relationship. In addition, by reducing the dosage of medication, they could demonstrate to themselves and their psychiatrist that they were neither dependent nor powerless, albeit that demonstration would be wordless and unconscious. I suggested to the patient that they were having a strong reaction to their psychiatrist's absence and recommended not immediately reducing the medication. The patient accepted that suggestion and, when their psychiatrist returned, decided not to change the dosage.

In addition to concerns about dependency, the psychotherapist-pharmacotherapist split is frequently reflected in issues of control or fears of being damaged by known and unknown long-term side effects. Both may reflect displacement of concerns about the therapist's hurtfulness and deeply unconscious fears of their own destructiveness. Patients may experience shame that is rooted in a belief that "needing" medication is a sign of weakness and fears that taking medication is inherently a sign of a serious condition, which, of course, it sometimes is. Patients who are insistent on pharmacotherapy, alone, may hope that the medication can transform them without their becoming aware of or exploring the troubling aspects of their minds or developing an intimate relationship with a psychotherapist.

Therapists also have conflicts that frequently interfere with an accurate assessment of the benefits of pharmacotherapy. Medication may symbolize the therapist's inadequacy, a state of mind often reflected in their indirectly boasting by emphasizing that the patient improved "without medication." Therapists may not want to "share" the patient's improvement with the medication. They may believe that alleviation of psychic distress by medication will reduce the patient's ability to make themselves vulnerable enough to explore difficult, anxiety-provoking material.

Pharmacotherapy, alone, or in combination with an additional kind of psychotherapy, creates an unavoidable and unresolvable ambiguity. Often, neither patient, pharmacotherapist, nor psychotherapist can know for certain what has caused a specific change. Some changes are clearly the result of known medication side effects, but the cause of many cannot be determined. Is the improvement in mood secondary to the pharmacological impact of the medication, a positive relationship with the pharmacotherapist, a placebo response (Spiro 1986, Moerman 2002) which is an aspect of the patient/pharmacotherapist relationship, or the psychotherapy?

Patients are frequently certain of the cause of changes when the pharmacotherapist or psychotherapist is not. To one degree or another, "I'm sure" reflects the patient's wish that it is the medication or the impact of psychotherapy that accounts for their improvement. Patients with a strong reluctance to take any medication may be conveying fear regarding developments in their relationship with the psychotherapist. Because the prescription of medication in the treatment of psychiatric disorders has become so prevalent and is so often expected, at some point in the initial meetings with patients, I will explore their thoughts and feelings about pharmacotherapy.

David I Joseph MD

<><><><><><><><><><><><><><><><><><><><><><><><><><><><><>

THE DSM REPRESENTS A NEW MYTH OF MENTAL ILLNESS.

In 1973, by a vote of its members (58% supported the change), the American Psychiatric Association decided that homosexuality was no longer a psychiatric disorder, a decision that unequivocally declared that psychiatry is, in its very essence, a biopsychosociocultural science. This perspective, which had been thoughtfully articulated by Adolf Meyer at Johns Hopkins from 1910–1940 and by George Engel at Rochester in the 1970s, conceptualized psychiatry as the field of medicine that encompassed the biological, psychological, and sociocultural influences on the human brain, mind, and behavior.

In 1980, after a six-year gestation and difficult labor, DSM III was born and radically changed the process of psychiatric diagnosis, shifting dramatically away from the subjectivity of DSM II and establishing objective criteria that determined a patient's diagnosis. The number of diagnoses in the DSM increased with each edition, from 106 in DSM I to nearly 500 in DSM V, and the creation of DSM V was marked with intense controversy (Frances, A., 2013; Greenberg, G., 2013; Horwitz, A. V., 2021). Paul Chodoff expressed (in personal communications) that he thought the DSM III was "medicalizing the human condition."

Eight years later, the psychiatrist and anthropologist Arthur Kleinman (1988) distinguished between a patient's illness and their disease. Illness is "the innately human experience of symptoms and suffering. Illness refers to how the sick person and the members of the family or wider social network perceive, live with, and respond to symptoms and disability." (3) Disease "is what the practitioner creates in the recasting of illness in terms of theories of disorder.... The practitioner reconfigures the patient's and family's illness problems as narrow technical issues, disease problems.... Disease is the problem from the practitioner's perspective. In the narrow biological terms of the biomedical model, this means that disease is reconfigured *only* as an alteration in biological structure or functioning." (5-6)

It is as though Kleinman's book was a response to the two events and was intended to provide a way of integrating these two aspects of psychiatric disorders, an integration that privileged neither the neurobiological nor the psychological perspective.

In 1961, Thomas Szasz published *The Myth of Mental Illness*, challenging the very notion that psychiatric conditions, even the most severe, were illnesses at all, a premise that seems hard to take seriously today. In some ways, by privileging reliability over validity, objectivity over subjectivity, and, implicitly, diagnosis over understanding and hearing over listening, I believe that the current DSM comes close to creating a mythology of its own.

The thorny problem of psychiatric diagnosis is not the focus of my concern. Rather, I wish to highlight the impact of the DSM III on how psychiatrists and other physicians—as well as all mental health professionals—conceptualize psychiatric disorders, and how this conceptualization influences their treatment of and relationship with patients.

It bears emphasizing that, much as we might wish otherwise, none of the diagnoses in DSM V is based on an anatomic, metabolic, or physiologic cause. The compelling allure of objectivity and pathology relating to the brain is, sometimes demeaningly, contrasted with the ambiguous quicksand of subjectivity regarding disturbances of the mind. This temptation persists despite the fact that many medical diseases, especially those involving pain, have a strong subjective component, and that the mind's adaptation to stress has a powerful influence on the development and course of many diseases.

The DSM has had a profound impact on all medical and mental health professions. The DSM "sets the boundary between normal and mental illness" and "has gained a huge social significance and determines all sorts of important things that have an enormous impact on people's lives—like who is considered well and who is sick; what treatment is offered; who pays for it; who gets disability benefits; who is eligible for mental health, school, vocational and other services; who gets to be hired for a job, can adopt a child or pilot a plane or qualifies for life insurance; whether a murderer is a criminal or a mental patient; what should be the damages awarded in lawsuits; and much, much more" (Frances 2013, xii).

The impact of the DSM is not limited to psychiatrists. "All mental health clinicians have been trained using the DSM categorical system.... Psychology, psychiatry, and social work textbooks are organized using these diagnostic conceptualizations, practice guidelines have been developed based on these categories, and epidemiological data, service use and medical economic data, outcome data, and so forth have been compiled based on these categories" (First, 2005, 562). Medical students are introduced to psychiatry through the DSM, and one study found that 80% of psychiatric medications are written by physicians who have no further psychiatric education or experience after medical school (Mark, T.I, Levit, K.R., and Buck, J.A. 2009).

The DSM is only one among many factors that have contributed to profound changes in psychiatric health care. Advances in psychiatric genetics, neuroimaging, neurobiology, and psychopharmacology, the commercialization of medicine, the pervasive influence of the pharmaceutical industry, the woefully inadequate insurance coverage of psychiatric disorders, and the isolation of most psychoanalytic institutes from the university have all contributed to the transformation of psychiatric thought and practice.

Contemporary medical practice allows too little time to speak with patients and fewer "hands on" interactions between patient and physician, depriving the patient of the healing impact of physical touch. In psychiatry and the other mental health disciplines, changes in our health care system make it less likely that our patients will feel "touched" by us. Without this kind of touch, the healing impact of our work is significantly diminished.

In reflecting on medical education, Kleinman (1988) noted that "Physicians are encouraged to believe that *disease* is more important than *illness*, and that all they need is knowledge about biology, not knowledge about the psychosocial and cultural aspects of illness. They are taught that using placebo effects in the clinical setting is old-fashioned. They come to believe that psychotherapy is anachronistic and need be learned only by psychiatrists. The social science and humanities components of medical education ... are poor relations with whom few medical students feel at all comfortable associating.... The gauntlet of residency training may even dehumanize the practitioner, and certainly does not contribute to the training of physicians committed to psychosocially sensitive care." (255) Now, some 40 years after his avowedly "harsh" conclusions, I am concerned that psychiatry itself, and to a lesser degree other mental health disciplines, are well described in the same terms.

David I Joseph MD

THOUGHTS AND BEHAVIORS SEEM IRRATIONAL BECAUSE WE DO NOT UNDERSTAND THEIR RATIONALE.

Morton Reiser (1988), a distinguished psychoanalyst, researcher, and chair of the Department of Psychiatry at Yale, wrote a seminal article: "Are psychiatric educators 'losing the mind'?" As the title suggests, the strong emphasis on the brain and objectivity and the deemphasis of mind and subjectivity have contributed to the waning of our understanding that all thoughts, emotions, and behaviors derive from a personal evaluation of the world and oneself. Thoughts, feelings, and actions—those of others as well as our own—often appear completely irrational, incomprehensible, devoid of logic, and beyond understanding. (In what follows, I am not referring to individuals intoxicated by PCP or other substances, although their thoughts, feelings and actions may well express meaning.) A man who believes his gastrointestinal tract is infested with maggots may simply be considered psychotic without any understanding that his unshakable belief reflects a deep-seated conviction that his self is rotten to the core and warrants only disgust, revulsion, and elimination.

In my first year of psychiatric residency, a young woman was admitted to the ward, intensely agitated, speaking with fragmented speech, and unable to provide a coherent history. She paced furiously around the ward, tightly wrapped in her raincoat which she would suddenly remove, revealing that she was wearing only a lacy bra and underpants. Until antipsychotic medication had taken hold, she repeated this process of disrobing, a pattern that appeared both carefully orchestrated and incomprehensible. Later, after her psychosis had resolved, she explained that she did not know who was going to visit her. If her mother arrived, she wanted to be in conservative clothing, but if her boyfriend came, she wanted to be dressed seductively. Not the best solution to her dilemma, to be sure, but one that had its own, completely understandable rationale.

In the course of her psychotherapy, a woman with a constant, inexplicable dread of church bells discovered, with shock, relief, and profound sadness and guilt, that her response to church bells resulted from their association with the death of her brother who had been killed by a car at noon while they were playing on the sidewalk. The bells were tolling at the time of the accident, and her response to this tragedy had been largely displaced and condensed into her dread of church bells. She had no conscious connection between her dread and her brother's tragic death, nor was she aware of the guilt stemming from the elimination of her rival and fear that she was responsible for his death. Far from irrational, her dread was completely logical.

The understanding that a patient's signs and symptoms have meaning has gradually eroded in contemporary psychiatric practice. A schizophrenic man who hears threatening voices accusing him of being a homosexual is conveying his own deeply dreaded, highly conflicted, unconscious homosexual longings. A manic woman's pressured speech, grandiosity, and flight of ideas is a desperate attempt to avoid her deep sadness and devalued sense of self, a self of which she is unaware and would adamantly deny. An obsessive-compulsive person's incessant hand washing may express a powerful, unconscious sense of a contaminated self, and a man who hears voices telling him that he is Christ may well be conveying his deep sense of personal inadequacy and unworthiness.

A successful attorney obsessively underwent repeated plastic surgery to remove insignificant facial blemishes. The plastic surgeon's reluctance to perform the surgery was met with increased pressure from the patient. Only when we discovered that this behavior was driven by his hidden, "ugly" sexual fantasies, did the desire for surgery decrease. All of the above examples would have been clear to most psychiatrists and psychotherapists in the past, but my recent experience supervising psychiatric residents suggests that it may well come as a surprise to many psychiatrists and psychotherapists today.

The hypothesis that the signs and symptoms of our patients have meaning does not imply that psychoanalytic psychotherapy will be the most effective treatment. In fact, some disorders—severe obsessive-compulsive disorder and eating disorders, to name two—are usually not responsive to such treatment and are much more effectively addressed by cognitive behavioral psychotherapy or a specialized treatment program, often in combination with pharmacotherapy. Psychotic disorders, incapacitating depression, mania, and crippling anxiety disorders are other conditions in which pharmacotherapy is usually required to alleviate symptoms and enable the patient to participate meaningfully in psychotherapy, whatever the type.

In the course of psychotherapy, psychotic patients may come to understand that they have distorted reality; depressed patients and patients with panic attacks may come to realize that, regardless of their genetic and biological predisposition, their inexplicable symptoms have definite, understandable precipitants; distrustful patients may come to see that their suspicions are rooted in understandable experiences and reflect their distrust of themselves. But this increased self-awareness comes at an unavoidable cost.

The psychotic patient must accept that they have, in fact, been psychotic—a frightening realization. The "irrational" patient who discovers the existence of their hidden rationality must confront what they have so successfully hidden from themselves. The distrustful patient will most certainly be relieved that their therapist is in their corner, yet they must come to terms with the far-reaching consequences of their suspiciousness and grieve how deeply it has permeated their being. They will also have to endure the sadness and guilt of knowing how their distrustfulness has affected their therapy, their therapist, and other important people in their life.

After a thorough neurological evaluation did not identify an organic explanation for disabling headaches, a 40-year-old man reluctantly agreed to a psychiatric consultation. As our initial meeting was drawing to a close, I had little idea of what, if anything, might be psychologically contributing to his headaches and suggested that we meet again. Politely, but without hesitation or ambivalence, he declined, emphatically stating that he would rather have a brain tumor than need to see a psychiatrist. Whatever he was hiding from me and from himself must have been so horrific that he would rather have cancer of the brain than cancer of the mind.

The rationale of some inexplicable or psychotic behavior may never be determined, but beginning each clinical relationship with the premise that a rationale does exist conveys deep respect for the patient's humanness and creates a relationship that has the potential for discovery and meaningful change. Assuming that there is reason to be found also provides wordless reassurance to the patient that their mind is not broken.

Every term which implies that a patient's mind is ill or their thinking is irrational contributes to a denigrating rather than respectful sense of otherness in the mind of the therapist and has a corrosive impact on the therapeutic relationship. I often recall Harry Stack Sullivan's (1953) unadorned, deeply meaningful reminder: "In most general terms, we are all much more simply human than otherwise, be we happy and successful, contented and detached, miserable and mentally disordered or whatever." From this perspective, the teaching of "psychopathology" is unfortunate, implying a negative sense of otherness, but I have been unable to discover or devise a better term.

◇◇

THE CLINICAL CONSULTATION IS THE BRIEFEST PSYCHOTHERAPY.

A clinical consultation, whether conducted in the emergency room, hospital ward, or personal office, is an extremely condensed psychotherapy. In this unique psychotherapy, patient and therapist develop a relationship, arrive at a shared understanding of the patient's most immediate problem, and determine a plan for treatment. Conducting an initial evaluation, regardless of the setting, requires a clinician to keep foremost in mind that a successful evaluation will depend on their ability to develop a working relationship with the patient, an outcome that is most likely to develop when the clinician demonstrates empathy, tact, and respect. Since all patients approach an initial consultation with significant apprehension and a range of expectations, the clinician needs to learn how the patient has approached the evaluation and how they are reacting to this initial meeting. Even in this first, and sometimes only, encounter, the clinician must remain attuned to any reactions the patient has to them.

Does the patient bring a persecutory perspective and believe that the clinician wants to have power over them, an experience especially common in the emergency room? Is the patient afraid that the clinician will be overly frightened by the depth of their depression and thoughts of suicide and will automatically recommend or require hospitalization? Are they deeply ashamed of seeking treatment and, if so, what does this concern reflect? Are they present only because a spouse has threatened divorce unless they address their alcoholism?

Whether, when, and how to address reactions to the therapist in the initial interview requires considerable tact, but addressing these reactions in an initial consultation can further understanding and contribute importantly to developing a mutual plan of treatment and solid therapeutic alliance (Ogden 1992).

If a clinician concludes that the patient should be hospitalized against their will, a tense struggle about the use of power dominates the situation for both. The issue appears clear: will the clinician use their power to hospitalize the patient? But the situation is actually more nuanced. In this most challenging situation, by exercising control over the patient's autonomy, the psychiatrist is acting for that aspect of the patient who does not wish to kill themselves or someone else. On some level, the patient is relieved that someone has intervened to protect them from acting on their frightening, destructive wishes. Not that any relief is expressed or even conscious. Most often it is totally disavowed, and the patient experiences only bitter resentment at the psychiatrist's "unwarranted" exercise of authority.

Though they lack this perspective in the moment, a patient who harms others also inflicts significant damage to themselves and their sense of self. In addition to any serious legal consequences, they will have irrevocably scarred their relationships with others and will (with the exception of the sociopathic patient) be haunted by pervasive guilt. Faced with needing to make an immediate decision, a therapist may be unable to focus on the fact that, were their deep hurt and rage to subside, the patient might have considerable conflict about putting their violent wishes into action. I have also found it helpful to keep in mind that the patient has the responsibility to engender in me the conviction that it is safe for treatment to occur on an outpatient basis. Another psychiatrist might not be as concerned as I, but in the moment, that is irrelevant. The decision about involuntary hospitalization is solely mine.

Since a successful clinical evaluation is a brief psychotherapy, the end of the evaluation warrants attention, limited though it may be. Reactions to the end of a consultation are especially strong when patients are evaluated by one clinician and referred to another. Patients who are screened by more senior staff to determine if they are "appropriate" for a clinician in training will understandably have a strong reaction to being referred to someone less experienced. Consultations undertaken with the understanding that the patient will be referred to another clinician put patient and therapist in a difficult situation. If the consultation is successful, the patient feels understood, respected, and relieved and has developed a meaningful relationship with the therapist. Referral to another clinician will therefore elicit meaningful disappointment, disappointment that is not alleviated by understanding at the outset that a referral would be made.

In such situations, ending the consultation may elicit a stronger reaction than one might expect. Should a transition to another clinician seem effortless and devoid of a sense of any disappointment, either the consultation will not have been very successful, or clinician and patient will have avoided the experience of an ending. Commonly the patient's reaction to the ending will result in failure to meet with the "replacement" therapist.

When, following a period of consultation, patient and therapist continue working together, an ending of sorts has also occurred, not dramatic, but significant nonetheless. The beginning of psy-chotherapy entails therapist and patient inhabiting different roles than they did during the evaluation. A friend in training to become a psychoanalyst told me that, at the end of the consultation, his analyst said, "Do you have any questions because, once we have started analysis, I will not answer any questions." While extreme, the principle of this analyst emphasizes that consultation psy-chotherapy and ongoing psychotherapy differ in significant ways. Learning more about the patient's medical, familial, historical, and developmental history is not among the immediate objec-tives of an ongoing psychotherapy. To a much greater degree, the psychoanalytic psychotherapist provides structure primarily by listening, allowing the patient to talk freely about whatever is on their mind, and acts primarily to decrease the patient's sense of vulnerability, thus enabling them to speak more spontaneously and openly. While it is generally not necessary to explain these changes in detail, keeping them in mind and being attuned to the patient's reactions to the changes will facilitate the transition.

~~~~~~

BETTER TO INVITE A PATIENT TO SHARE THEIR STORY THAN TO TAKE THEIR HISTORY.

All clinicians, but especially physicians, understand that an initial task is to "take the patient's history." "Taking" a history, however, implies a relationship in which the clinician extracts something from the patient. A series of questions from the clinician and answers given (or withheld) by the patient shapes the kind of relationship they will develop. By contrast, inviting a patient to share their story contributes to a relationship in which the therapist develops a deeper, richer, more nuanced understanding of the patient, and patient and therapist initiate their relationship with a very different beginning. It is worth remembering that, in the course of a meaningful psychoanalysis, all patients will understand their histories very differently just as they will develop a new, richer understanding of themselves (Schafer 1994).

How much history is necessary to develop an initial plan of treatment depends on situational constraints and, of course, histories are never complete, just as psychoanalytic psychotherapy is never truly finished. The patient brings to the evaluation a particular problem and private suffering, seeking a solution to the problem and relief from the pain. The clinician brings to the evaluation a framework of basic information that they need to acquire to develop an initial plan of treatment and a desire to develop some initial understanding of the patient's suffering. The tightly organized approach that all psychiatrists learned in medical school and that has been adopted to some degree by other mental health professionals, sacrifices a more balanced, mutually created therapeutic alliance in order to reach "a diagnosis" and develop a plan of treatment more rapidly.

A successful clinical consultation will be comprised of as many sessions as it needs. While this flexibility is possible in the private setting, in outpatient clinics, health maintenance organizations, other similar entities, and most dramatically in the emergency room, the clinician is required to arrive at a diagnosis and plan of treatment, sometimes after only a single meeting. However, even in such situations, how a patient chooses to present their history conveys facts of a very different kind than those learned via question and answer.

When asked what brought him to see me, Mr. C began by saying that he was a very busy attorney at a prestigious law firm. It wasn't until later in the meeting that he shared the reason he had called. He was depressed and frightened by periodic suicidal fantasies. By emphasizing his professional success at the outset, without realizing it, he had informed me about a private sense of weakness and inadequacy, concerns over possible threats to his professional stature, and great distress that his intense sadness had shaken his own self-respect and self-confidence. Implicitly he also conveyed a concern that he was ashamed to be meeting and, if he allowed me to know him, I, too, would lose respect for him. This completely unremarkable experience reflects the significant impact of allowing the patient to shape the beginning of the consultation; questions can be saved for later.

◇◇◇◇◇◇◇◇◇◇◇◇◇◇◇◇◇◇◇◇◇◇◇◇◇◇◇◇◇◇

ALL PSYCHOLOGICAL SYMPTOMS HAVE PRECIPITANTS—MANY ALSO HAVE MEANING.

Patients who can vividly describe their emotional distress are frequently unaware of any event that precipitated their anxiety, depression, or other symptoms. Furthermore, free-floating anxiety and some other diagnoses are described and defined in a manner implying that there may well be no precipitant, whatsoever. As one man told me in our first meeting: "The panic just comes over me." In time, psychoanalytic therapy will usually reveal that symptoms are a response to an identifiable, unconscious stimulus, one which the patient finds deeply unsettling.

Any number of undiagnosed biological illnesses may present with signs and symptoms indistinguishable from disorders solely of psychological origin. Since hereditary and biological factors frequently contribute to an increased vulnerability to anxiety, loss, shame, or aggression, a stimulus which might seem relatively insignificant can have a profound, intense impact on the patient. Free-floating anxiety represents a condition in which the stimulus and the response have become unconsciously separated within the mind. The patient is being completely honest when they are certain that there is no "reason" for their anxiety, sadness, irritability, etc., or attributes it entirely to a gene inherited from an anxious parent.

Respecting the importance of precipitants has significant implications for treatment. Ignoring their role leaves the patient with no sense of control, rendering them completely vulnerable to factors outside themselves. They may learn how to adapt more effectively to their distress, but identifying and understanding precipitating factors and the reasons for their impact will facilitate greater change.

Even patients with the most severe psychiatric disorders need to identify situations that may be disorganizing. Intense emotion of any kind is often threatening and destabilizing for a schizo-phrenic patient, and this understanding can be integrated into a plan of treatment in which patient and family develop techniques for limiting the level of expressed emotion.

Since most patients have been suffering for a considerable time before seeking treatment, it is important to determine why the patient called when they did. Even a stimulus that seems inconse-quential provides a meaningful window into a central aspect of the patient's vulnerability. A middle-aged woman had often considered seeking treatment for her long-standing alcohol abuse, but it was only when her husband threatened to leave her that her dread of being alone led her to call a therapist. Not surprisingly, her fear of aloneness and abandonment engendered very powerful reactions to the absence of any important person, including the therapist.

"WHY NOT SOONER" PROVIDES UNDERSTANDING OF THE LEADING EDGE OF VULNERABILITY.

A corollary to exploring the specific precipitant of a patient's decision to request an initial appointment focuses on understanding what kept them from seeking treatment sooner. Interest in the patient's postponement of care—or in cases where the patient is brought to the emergency room involuntarily, their avoidance of treatment altogether—will highlight what I have come to think as psychological "point tenderness." Point tenderness is a medical term that refers to the exquisite, precisely located pain of acute appendicitis, but in this context, it resides within the mind. To paraphrase Thomas Ogden (1988), it is the patient's leading edge of vulnerability.

Listening for the leading edge of vulnerability is meaningful for each patient in every clinical situation, but it is especially important in the initial hour of consultation. The leading edge of vulnerability is the particular psychological area where, at the moment, the patient feels most exposed, most ashamed, most concerned about being hurt in some manner. It is where they are most vulnerable and most desirous of relief.

Whether conscious or not, concerns that lead patients to avoid treatment will powerfully shape their initial meeting with a therapist. A young man's aggressive behavior prompted his frightened parents to bring him to the hospital. He knew that he had alarmed his parents but avoided treatment precisely because he dreaded being hospitalized involuntarily and having his release be determined by others. For him, the leading edge of vulnerability was rooted in his fear of being controlled by others in whom he had little or no trust. On a deeper level, he dreaded that he could not regulate how he expressed his fury. Clues to the leading edge of vulnerability are often more subtle. Well into his initial session, a man in his 20s began conveying in detail how much time he devoted to exercise and weight lifting, an indication that he postponed seeking treatment because he feared and was deeply ashamed of being feminine and feared his sexual attraction to men.

As my colleagues Dominic Mazza and Bob Winer have stressed (personal communication), an important goal of an initial consultation is that the patient will wish to return for a second appointment, an outcome that will be more likely to be achieved if they feel understood, respected, and safe. Paying close attention to the patient's explanation for postponing or avoiding treatment will further this outcome. Many patients present with their suffering both apparent and freely expressed, but such an introduction can readily lead the therapist to minimize how vulnerable every patient feels. Particularly in the initial meeting, vulnerability exists alongside great relief in having unburdened themselves, begun to establish a trusting relationship, and developed hope for alleviating their distress.

Sometimes the answer to "why not sooner" does not become apparent for a surprisingly long time, a situation in which I need to remind myself that each patient has met with me to alleviate their distress, conscious or deeply buried. A middle-aged lobbyist sought consultation because her internist thought that something psychological might be contributing to her irritable bowel syndrome that was reasonably well controlled with medication. Happily married, the mother of three adult children, she was approaching the age at which she was expected gradually to reduce her hours at work so that younger colleagues could assume greater responsibility.

The patient relayed a number of experiences in her childhood that must have been difficult and stressful but gave no indication that they elicited any psychological distress, either during her childhood or as she relayed her life history to me. My inquiry into why she had not sought a consultation sooner indicated that she felt no need to consult a psychiatrist and had seen me only at the urging of her internist. Somewhat to my surprise, after several meetings, she readily accepted my suggestion that we meet regularly, which we did for many years. Well into treatment, she mentioned, with no affect or awareness of its importance, that her father had been a survivor of the Holocaust, a topic that had never been discussed within the family and that I had absolutely no reason to have suspected.

I privately hypothesized that the prospect of being forced to retire resonated powerfully with the impact of the Holocaust on her and her family, but I have no evidence to confirm or disconfirm this speculation. I cite this experience to highlight that inquiring "why not sooner" may sometimes fail to identify an event or a private experience, but in these instances, one should be alert to a traumatic event whose impact the patient has unconsciously buried for many years.

◇◇◇◇◇◇◇◇◇◇◇◇◇◇◇◇◇◇◇◇◇◇◇◇◇◇◇◇◇◇◇◇◇◇◇

CHEMICAL IMBALANCES ARE THE SPICES OF LIFE.

Understanding that a psychiatric disorder is caused by a "chemical imbalance" is both a painfully obvious truth and a dangerously simplistic, misleading perspective. Our very aliveness is defined by constantly shifting states of mind, each with neurophysiological, biochemical, and psychological attributes that are responses of the body, brain, and mind to various stimuli. These stimuli can be external or internal, emotional or cognitive, and are influenced by biological, psychological, and sociocultural factors.

The chemical balance of our minds is reflected in the ever-changing moods, intellectual enterprises, and infinite varieties of states of aliveness, including sleep, that we experience throughout the day. Boredom reflects a state of mind in which the experience of chemical imbalance has been greatly reduced and one's sense of balance seems only marginally altered throughout the day. In my experience, boredom often obscures a cauldron of intensity. Most often, shifts in the chemical balance of our mind do not cause us to lose our mental balance; to the contrary, we embrace and enjoy them when they are pleasurable, and respect and accept them when they are painful or provoke anxiety.

From this perspective, psychiatric disease and psychiatric illness reflect conditions in which an individual has lost their mental balance and has been unable to regain it. In these situations, the adaptive mechanisms, psychological and biological, which the patient has utilized and depended upon over their lifetime have not allowed them to achieve mastery over their internal state of mind and regain their chemical and psychological equilibrium. The intensity of the patient's emotion, be it fear, anxiety, sorrow, fury or sexual desire, has overwhelmed their ability to maintain homeostasis.

Ironically, such an individual is often deeply concerned that they are "too much" for others, yet lack the awareness that they have become "too much" for themselves, both physically and psychologically. Patients with characterological difficulties have adapted to a deeply frightening loss of psychological balance in childhood by adapting in ways that allow recovery of their psychological balance, albeit at a considerable cost. The patient's conscious experience of distress may have been reduced, but balance has been achieved at the cost of psychological flexibility.

Understanding "chemical imbalance" from this perspective does not devalue genetic predisposition, inborn constitution, medical illness, or the advisability of pharmacotherapy. This perspective does provide a metaphor for understanding and addressing the patient's distress. Such a perspective reflects the fact that the patient's clinical condition, however it presents, reflects their inability to regain balance following a painful loss, fear of a possible "catastrophe," and myriad other psychological or physical precipitants. For extremely vulnerable individuals such as those prone to road rage, a seemingly insignificant stimulus can precipitate an extreme response, and sometimes they are unable to regain their balance before some tragic consequence has occurred.

Many psychiatric disorders are commonly conceptualized by

the medical profession, the mental health community, and by the wider public as evidence that a "chemical imbalance" has been created by some force outside the person's mind—a force acting on their brain. In seeking help, patients are seeking assistance to regain their psychological balance and to rectify the biochemical and neurophysiological changes associated with it. One goal of psychotherapy is to help the patient learn new ways of maintaining their balance in stressful situations so that they are less likely to be knocked off kilter by situations that have repeatedly elicited unsettling reactions. If effective, longer-term psychotherapy will also assist the patient to respond less powerfully to stimuli that have elicited deep distress.

At the risk of repetition, it is always important to keep in mind that a patient's loss of emotional balance is frequently a manifestation of a neurological illness or other disease. A man in his 90s had been in a very productive psychotherapy as a young man for significant anxiety and sought consultation with me because of an uneasy tension, unrelated to any particular concern. He had been recently evaluated by his internist and was being monitored continuously for atrial fibrillation.

We met weekly for some time, and, while it was clear that aging and thoughts of dying were contributing to his anxiety, I left each meeting with the nagging concern that something was missing, a hunch that was confirmed when it was discovered that the electronic monitoring of his atrial fibrillation had not been functioning for some time, and his cardiac status had deteriorated significantly. Only when this was rectified did his anxiety subside. This experience of the impact of body on mind was reinforced when I ran across a report (*Science News* 2023) of an experiment in which mice, whose heart rate was increased electronically while all other variables remained unchanged, became clinically anxious.

David I Joseph MD

◇◇

A GOOD THERAPEUTIC RELATIONSHIP IS THE BEST "MEDICATION."

Patients have little reason to expect that developing a trusting, supportive relationship with a therapist will be a very effective anti-anxiety and anti-depressant agent, an agent that will facilitate the reestablishment and maintenance of their physiological and psychological balance. This relationship is the foundation of the placebo response (Spiro 1986; Moerman 2002). How best to conceptualize the therapeutic alliance and how best to facilitate its development has been debated for some time. Charles Brenner (1979), Ralph Greenson (1965), and Elizabeth Zetzel (1970) hold different perspectives on the subject, but all clinicians understand that developing a trusting, safe relationship with the patient is essential.

Although important in the ongoing treatment of acute psychosis, schizophrenia, bipolar disorder, severe depression, and crippling anxiety disorders, a positive therapeutic alliance, by itself, very rarely ameliorates disabling symptoms for these patients. For most other disorders, and sometimes for major depression and severe anxiety, the impact of a positive experience during the initial evaluation meeting can alleviate symptoms, often to a startling degree. When a patient leaves an initial meeting having experienced the therapist's care, has felt listened to, and feels trust has been established, the newly established relationship ameliorates the patient's isolation, fear, despair, and hopelessness. That relationship has changed the patient's internal world, physical and psychological; it has facilitated their regaining psychological and neurobiological balance.

I have found it very meaningful to conceptualize the psychotherapeutic relationship from an "organic" perspective. The therapist ingests and absorbs every aspect of the patient: words, tone, somatic expressions, silences, etc., and then metabolizes them, formulates an initial understanding of the patient's concern and vulnerability, and creates a response—sometimes primarily listening—that alleviates the patient's distress. The patient takes in, or sometimes insistently and persistently rejects, the therapist's words, affects, ideas, interpretations, consistency, empathy, concern, etc. They digest, absorb, and metabolize them, and use them to regain their equilibrium.

If the psychotherapy continues, they are gradually able to use their ever-deepening self-awareness and understanding to transform their sense of self. When a patient gains significant relief from an initial meeting, some psychological nutrients which had been missing were provided to them by the therapist and used to reestablish a sense of balance and perspective. Ongoing psychotherapy, if productive and transformative, facilitates changes within the patient such that events or stimuli that so disturbed them and brought them to treatment do not have the same deeply unsettling and unmanageable effects. Travel may still elicit apprehension, sorrow may still elicit anxiety, anger may remain difficult to manage, but the challenges will be reduced and the ability to adapt to them in more productive ways will have become very much part of the person.

At the conclusion of an initial meeting with a patient, I cannot predict the impact of our new relationship. For this reason, I rarely prescribe any medication during an initial meeting. Only patients who are psychotic, manic, severely depressed, or disabled by anxiety merit the immediate introduction of pharmacotherapy. Patients have been living with their distress for many months and sometimes years prior to meeting with us; continuing to endure it for a short period of time will not be overly burdensome or hurtful.

Not prescribing medication after an initial contact with a patient ought not preclude acknowledging the deep suffering the patient has endured. For patients in significant distress, I make certain to meet with them the next day or as soon as possible thereafter. Delaying the decision about the prescription of medication reduces the patient's sense of urgency and allows patient and therapist to assess the impact of establishing a treatment relationship. I have been profoundly surprised by outcomes at both ends of the spectrum: the patient whose profound depression was significantly alleviated by an initial meeting, and the moderately anxious person who got absolutely no symptomatic relief from an initial consultation that I believed had been extremely helpful.

A mother's relationship with an infant and young child is one template for understanding the importance of and impact of the therapeutic relationship. Ideally, a mother responds to her child's needs and distress with concern, empathy, physical comfort, feeding, and reassurance, much of it wordless. But, unless it is warranted, fear and anxiety are not among her reactions.

The mother's soothing, concerned yet unalarmed response assists the child's ability to endure the distress and facilitates its resolution. Repeated a myriad of times, the child develops an ever-stronger ability to self-regulate in times of suffering. How often have we experienced a crying child cease floods of tears once a bandage has been lovingly applied? The field of mother-infant observation (Benveniste 2021) is based on the belief that such an experience will sharpen the therapist's observational and listening skills and facilitate the therapist's effectiveness.

One of my supervisors, psychoanalyst Arnold Meyersburg, frequently worked with patients considered too severely impaired for analytic psychotherapy. He told me of his experience with a patient who became extremely agitated and began banging her head against the wall. He said that he went over to the couch, put his arm between the patient's head and the wall, and silently held her. After a brief period, she regained her composure.

At the time, I was most struck that he took a physical action; words were clearly not going to soothe her, and he was not concerned that his holding her would be seen as seductive or damage their therapeutic relationship. After several minutes, the patient was no longer as agitated and remarked, with wonder and relief, "Your heart isn't even beating fast." Dr. Meyersburg's interaction with this severely distressed patient embodies much that is central to a healing relationship between patient and therapist, just as it is central to a nurturing relationship between mother and child. If the caregiver is concerned but not anxious, the other person is reassured and soothed. There are, of course, clinical situations in which the therapist's anxiety is warranted and often necessary to protect the patient from acting in hurtful ways.

Especially when evaluating children, it is important to withhold pharmacotherapy until one has completed a very thorough evaluation of the child and the family. Common life experiences such as the birth of a sibling or going to school for the first time can trigger intense reactions that are difficult for the child to manage and are often associated with significant regression. The death of a parent or sibling, overt and frightening conflict within the family, fear of or the actual experience of violence, sexual abuse, and parental drug or alcohol use are more traumatic but not uncommon contributors to a child's disorder.

Childhood inattentiveness, often immediately assumed to reflect ADHD, deserves a careful, thorough evaluation to determine whether life events and family conflict have been significant contributors to the difficulty in concentration. Conceptualizing childhood enuresis or encopresis solely from the perspective of organic bladder or bowel disease is reductionistic and results in an inadequate evaluation and inadequate treatment. In addition, it is worth emphasizing that we are only beginning to understand the impact of medication on the developing brain and body, a fact which should give us additional pause before rushing to recommend psychotropic medication for children.

As explored earlier, prescribing medication during an initial meeting creates uncertainty. If medication is prescribed and the patient improves quickly, it is impossible to know to what degree the changes are a response to the pharmacological agent, the placebo response, the establishment of a positive working relationship, or a combination of these factors. If the response is positive, the patient should continue the medication for a considerable number of months, a not insignificant matter given the side effects of many medications. If the patient does not improve after several weeks, one cannot be certain whether continuing distress reflects pharmacological unresponsiveness, difficulties in establishing a therapeutic alliance, or both.

I have found the concept of psychotherapeutic parenting to be very meaningful. "Parenting," as it pertains to psychotherapy, does not involve treating the patient as a child or acting as the patient's parent. In fact, much of psychotherapeutic work involves understanding and working with the patient to refashion the ways in which they consider themselves to be a child looking for a parent. If parenting is understood to reflect a relationship in which one person relates to another in a way that furthers their growth, development, and maturation, then a psychotherapeutic relationship ought to be its own unique kind of parenting. Other writers, Loewald (1960) among them, have conceptualized the psychoanalyst as having achieved a more mature psychological level of development that facilitates the patient's transformation, a perspective that is consistent with the concept of psychoanalytic parenting.

◇◇

DEVELOPING A PLAN OF TREATMENT IS MORE EFFECTIVE THAN PRESCRIBING ONE.

The most productive plan of treatment emerges in an organic way from the process of the consultation and is clearly based on information that has been shared by the patient. This perspective is consistent with inviting the patient to relate their history rather than "taking it." An organically formulated treatment recommendation reflects mutuality but does not disavow the clinician's knowledge and expertise. If the recommendation has been based on what the patient has shared, it will not be experienced as a prescription offered by "the professional." The patient, whether or not they concur with the recommendation, ought not be surprised by anything the clinician says. Implicit in the above is the clinician's careful communication about what they have learned from the patient (and sometimes from others) and how that knowledge has led to their conclusions and recommendations.

A 40-year-old married man with several children repeatedly had intense conflict with his superiors at work and sought my opinion about whether he should again undertake psychotherapy. He said that he had been in treatment at least four times during his life but had been scornful and critical of each therapist and had ended treatment after less than a year. None of the psychotherapists had met with him more than once per week, and he had not found any of them to be at all helpful. Although he volunteered that he was bitterly disappointed with his brilliant but rather unsuccessful father and had been very much admired and celebrated by his mother, he displayed no understanding that the impact of his relationships with his parents was reflected in his scorn and lack of respect for his superiors at work and his therapists.

After several sessions, I said that I believed that he was perfectly able to make very good use of psychotherapy, but that, given his prior experiences, he would almost certainly soon find himself disappointed by and contemptuous of me and would be sorely tempted to fire me as he had his other therapists. I said that it would take time and meeting frequently for the two of us to understand what was motivating this pattern and to get a picture of how his relationship with me and his prior therapists was reflected in his long-standing difficulties at work. I added that he must have been extremely disappointed by his prior experiences with psychotherapy and would understandably be cautious about committing himself to yet another try.

The patient, being fully aware that everything I had said had been based on what he had shared, was relieved that I did not believe that his enduring difficulties were hopeless and that I thought he and I could work together productively. Having recognized the importance of the pattern of his previous psychotherapies and understanding its relevance to his professional difficulties, he had an inkling that he was not the unfortunate victim of several incompetent psychotherapists. He also appeared to understand that he and I were bound to encounter the same kind of intense conflict that had led him to abandon previous treatments. In response to my recommendation, he said that he thought he could work with me, and we began what developed into a productive psychotherapy, replete with challenging weeks when I was the object of his searing scorn, intense disappointment, and strong impulse to add me to his long list of disposable therapists.

In any outpatient psychotherapy, the clinician must decide what type and what dosage of psychotherapy is indicated, whether to include medication in the treatment, and whether additional interventions such as mindfulness and meditation or family therapy will be useful. Regardless of the type, psychotherapy will be an integral aspect of any ongoing relationship with the patient. At the risk of repeating myself, one cannot not be a psychotherapist. The constraints imposed on clinicians in HMOs and clinics, along with the significant limitations of most insurance policies, often place the clinician who believes that frequent sessions are necessary in a very difficult position. Either they agree to provide a level of care they consider inadequate or they commit themselves to a long, time-consuming, often fruitless struggle with the organization or insurance company to obtain permission for more frequent psychotherapeutic sessions.

I believe that the clinician has the ethical responsibility to inform the patient that the clinic or insurance company will not support the kind of treatment the clinician believes is indicated and necessary. Many clinicians have not been trained in nor had any experience with more intensive psychotherapies, and when forced to work within the constraints of weekly or less frequent sessions, come to believe that this frequency is not only adequate but desirable. I have met a number of therapists who consider weekly sessions to be intensive. Given their training, how could it be otherwise? Were this evolution not to occur, the clinician would be haunted by the conviction that they are providing inadequate care, an impossible situation. And so, it is scarcely surprising that many therapists gradually absorb and ratify the restrictions of the organization or insurance company. This is a variation of the Stockholm syndrome in which prisoners identify with their captors, only in this situation, both patients and clinicians are prisoners.

Given the constraints of contemporary mental health services and insurance coverage, developing conviction about what the patient requires is a difficult challenge. Patients in an acute situation usually need to be seen several days after the first session. Even those who do not absolutely "need" to be seen quickly will understand that the therapist who schedules a second visit close to the first understands their distress and takes it seriously. Patients who are not in acute distress will need to be seen as frequently as necessary to accomplish the goals of the therapy. That seems self-evident and simple enough but, given our medical and mental health care system, its implementation is often surprisingly complicated.

Although I am a psychoanalyst and believe that psychoanalysis is the treatment of choice for many patients, I do not recommend it by name. Rather, the patient and I arrive at a mutually desired frequency and an understanding that "freely associating" will further the work. Some patients wish to use the couch and find that it facilitates their speaking freely and spontaneously. Some wish to use the couch but find, often to their surprise and distress, that not seeing the therapist is disruptive and disorganizing. Some patients explicitly indicate that they do not want to lie on the couch, feeling exposed physically and distressed at being unable to gauge the therapist's physical response to them. If, after a period of meaningful work, a patient has not mentioned the couch or given any explanation for preferring to sit up, I wonder about its absence from our conversation. While I have recommended to some patients that using the couch will facilitate our work, I have never insisted on it.

As discussed earlier, every plan of treatment must include the decision about whether to initiate a course of medication. This decision will grow out of three factors: the degree to which the patient's symptoms are interfering with their psychological and physiological functioning, the clinician's opinion about how effectively and rapidly psychotherapy alone will lead to the amelioration of symptoms, and the patient's attitude toward medication. All psychotherapy involves learning. Severe anxiety, marked depression, psychosis, and other serious conditions are so disruptive to the patient's mental functioning that psychotherapy cannot be conducted unless combined with pharmacotherapy. Ameliorating symptoms pharmacologically is not the equivalent of anesthetizing the patient's emotional mind. If properly prescribed and managed, medication can markedly facilitate the work and efficacy of psychotherapy.

<><><><><><><><><><><><><><><><><><><><><><><>

THE UNLIKEABLE PATIENT IS SEEKING TREATMENT FOR THEIR UNLIKEABILITY.

At the conclusion of a consultation, therapists often inquire whether the patient would feel comfortable working with them. Equally important is whether the therapist believes they can work with the patient. I will not begin treatment with any patient who needs to explore and fully discuss an issue that I know will be so painful that I cannot be present in the way I would want and need to be. Although I am not a religious Jew, I would not choose to work with someone who was an active Nazi. I know that I could not be as empathically and personally present as the patient would need and deserve me to be, and to be candid, I would not want to try.

For the same reason, I do not think that a therapist who is unalterably opposed to abortion should work with a pregnant woman who is painfully wrestling with whether to end her pregnancy. Similarly, an African-American therapist should surely think twice before undertaking psychotherapy with an avowed racist. Sometimes, a current event in the therapist's life makes working with a specific patient too painful and therefore ill advised. If I had recently endured the death of one of my children, I would not work with a patient whose child was critically ill or had recently died.

Some analytic psychotherapists will not begin psychotherapy with someone whom they instantly and intensely dislike. This situation is cruelly ironic; these patients, whether they are aware of it or not, are undertaking therapy because of their unpleasantness and hope that the therapist can help them transform themselves into a more likable person. They also hope to change the powerful, deeply unconscious ways in which they do not like themselves. If the therapy is to be meaningful and productive, therapists know that they will, at some point, find themselves knee deep in the patient's nastiness, scorn, and sadism.

To initiate treatment with a person who announces that they are irritating and unpleasant is daunting to say the least. Knowing with certainty that they will be repeatedly engaged in tortured, sadomasochistic struggles, the therapist must decide whether they can experience the patient's attacks and still sustain an empathic, therapeutic treatment. The horror, disgust, anger, and fear inherent in work with perpetrators of domestic violence, child abuse, rape, or murder will be so intense that many therapists cannot work effectively with them. In my experience, these clinical dilemmas are quite common, although rarely discussed.

No matter how far reaching and transformative, a therapist's personal psychoanalysis cannot and ought not strive to create an emotionally invulnerable person. Ironically, undergoing personal analysis not only facilitates a greater ability to tolerate painful affects and thoughts but also contributes to becoming aware, often with considerable pain and surprise, of the ways in which one is forever vulnerable. A productive analysis may result in more effective adaptations to one's vulnerabilities, but vulnerabilities they remain. I remember well a senior psychoanalyst telling our residency class that he did not think he could work effectively with very attractive blonde women and always referred them to someone else. I doubt, however, that he told them why.

When grappling with the conundrum of an unlikeable patient,

I begin with the conviction that the patient's unlikeable qualities reflect the best adaptive response they can make to whatever severe stresses or traumas they have experienced. I believe that they know about their unlikeable self, suffer at the hands of it, and, regardless of the satisfactions it brings them, have a strong desire to change. In deciding whether to work with a patient I do not like, I try to determine whether I can find something genuinely likable about this person, something powerfully present that is obscured by the obnoxious, hateful aspects of their character. I also try hard to remember that, while I am certain that I will find it difficult to "live with them" as their analyst, they find it infinitely more difficult to live with themselves, something they have to do every hour of every day. If I can discover and retain this aspect of an unlikeable person, I will undertake psychotherapy with them, albeit with considerable trepidation.

Being ruthlessly honest about one's vulnerabilities will help to counter the ever-present threat of psychoanalytic omnipotence and facilitate a state of mind in which one can acknowledge: "Your suffering and difficulties deserve an empathic therapist, but I am not that person. I would, however, be glad to refer you to someone I know and respect." Regardless of tact and empathy, communicating this to a patient will be painful for therapist and patient, but I believe that such empathic honesty, even if difficult for therapist to convey and patient to hear, is both ethical and helpful to the patient.

CREATING A PSYCHOANALYTIC RELATIONSHIP, DEVELOPING A PSYCHOANALYTIC PROCESS

The aphorisms of the previous section were organized around factors inherent in initial consultations with a patient. This section considers issues central to initiating and conducting an ongoing psychotherapy.

◇◇◇

A PATIENT PAYING MORE OR LESS THAN THEY CAN AFFORD HARMS BOTH PATIENT AND THERAPIST.

For many psychiatrists and psychotherapists, negotiating a fee is an uncomfortable and infrequently discussed process. How rigorously should one explore the patient's financial resources? Should one inquire about savings, lifestyle, the financial status of parents? How can one make an informed decision about the fee without feeling like an agent of the Internal Revenue Service? Agreeing to a fee lower than the patient can afford may harm the patient by leading them to believe that they have gotten away with something, and it may also lead them to wonder whether the therapist has their own difficulties dealing with money. The therapist may harbor resentment that they have been shortchanged or may wrestle with their avoidance of negotiating a fee they believe is warranted.

Whenever a patient has a reduced fee, patient and therapist must grapple with difficult situations that are certain to occur. Early in my career, one of the four "control case" patients required by the institute was paying me a significantly reduced fee. His was my first appointment of the day, and one morning he arrived in an expensive car, never having mentioned that he was getting rid of his old one or any conflict, given his low fee, about how much to spend. He also did not give voice to any concern about my reaction. At that time, I was extremely apprehensive about discussing the issue at all. My institute required that one of my patients "complete" their analysis, and I feared that he might respond to my raising the issue of his car by quitting. In retrospect, I am convinced that my concerns were unwarranted, but I learned from my avoidance. Agreeing to a fee that "feels too low" is very likely to engender guilt in the patient and resentment in the therapist who will also know that they have devalued their psychoanalytic worth. In one way or another, the reactions of both will seep into the treatment.

Concern about greed may contribute to a therapist's discomfort negotiating the fee. When I was a psychoanalytic candidate, it was not uncommon for patients, especially psychoanalytic candidates, to take second jobs or secure a loan to finance their treatment. Given that one's personal therapy is the best investment one can make, both options seemed prudent and warranted. True, times were different then. Psychoanalysis was embraced by many departments of psychiatry, and insurance coverage for psychiatric care was often very generous.

How much sacrifice is warranted for the rewards of a meaningful analysis remains worthy of our consideration, although, in all candor, it has been many years since I knew of someone borrowing money to finance their treatment, much less a therapist's inquiring whether the patient has considered it. A therapist who feels uncomfortable or overly intrusive inquiring about the patient's finances should consider that their concerns may reflect the patient's wish to hold on to his money, to deprive the therapist, or some other motivation. In such situations, the therapist's discomfort has been engendered by the patient's unspoken relationship with money.

When a young adult or someone with a wealthy spouse wants to finance their treatment "on their own," the therapist is pulled in different directions. For young adults the fee and the question of parental assistance is a developmental issue. For the spouse whose husband or wife can well afford to support the treatment, the question of the fee offers a window into the nature of the marital relationship as well as the patient's concerns about autonomy and dependency.

In these circumstances, a thorough exploration of the struggle for independence from parents or spouse is necessary before reaching a decision about accepting a reduced fee. In most instances, I do not reduce the fee. To do so would reinforce the patient's conviction that they are too dependent on their parents or their spouse and protect the patient from experiencing financial indebtedness, a concern that almost certainly has to do with much more than money. A reduced fee also transfers the patient's unconscious concerns about becoming powerfully indebted to the therapist psychologically into very concrete terms about feeling indebted financially.

Some therapists do not raise the fee for patients they have seen for many years. This is another indication of how deeply personal an intense psychotherapeutic experience becomes for the therapist, and how the personal aspects of the relationship can impact the professional to such a degree that the professional aspect of the relationship is diluted. Not raising the fee for a patient for whom it is affordable suggests the therapist's concern that the deeply personal relationship, which has developed over years of intimate conversations and hard work, would be spoiled by respecting its professional aspects. Increasing the fee makes the professional aspect of the relationship all too concrete and too painfully apparent to both the patient and his therapist.

This was highlighted for me some years ago when I increased

the fee of a graduate analyst who had been meeting with me in supervision. Startled and momentarily speechless, he said that his analyst had never increased his fee, and he, assuming this was the psychoanalytic norm, had never increased the fee for any of his patients nor reflected on the significance of this way of managing the fee. He changed his policy on the spot, and I am certain that no supervisee of mine ever had a more profitable supervisory session.

Every analyst should formulate a clear policy regarding billing. I have always tried to give each patient their bill at the beginning of the first session of the month and tell each patient that I want to be paid by the 10th. The specifics of a policy regarding payment vary, but it is important that the analyst have a definite time when they expect to paid and to observe when patients are late in paying. When and how one makes a late payment an object to be explored will vary, but having a clear policy that one applies consistently allows the myriad issues that are played out around money to be brought into focus.

Early in my career, a young, married woman with a well-spring of hurt and anger, nervously told me that she would be several days late in paying my bill. When I inquired about the circumstances, she said that her checking account was low, but assured me that her husband's paycheck would be deposited in several days. She then volunteered that she did not want to borrow the funds from their savings account. She was quite taken aback when I observed that she was asking me to "borrow" the money rather than borrow it herself, and we engaged in a productive discussion of how she often felt deprived and wanted others to do things for her. This clinical experience would not have developed had I not maintained a consistent policy regarding payment.

<><><><><><><><><><><><><><><><><><><><><><><><><><><><>

ANY FINANCIAL POLICY REGARDING MISSED APPOINTMENTS IS ARBITRARY.

Every therapist has to develop a policy about whether to bill patients for missed sessions, and, in my experience, each policy is unique. My introduction to private practice coincided with the beginning of my psychoanalytic training, and, since my psychiatric residency completely ignored the myriad issues involved in administering a private practice, I was most influenced by instructors in the psychoanalytic institute. For the most part, each had the same policy. Once a regular schedule for analysis was established, the patient would be charged for every session, whether they attended or not. The reason for their absence never led to a decision not to charge for the session. I even learned of one analyst who billed a patient who was so anxious that they got lost on the way to their initial meeting. Not surprisingly, the patient did not return and did not pay the bill. I never learned if my instructors had the same policy for patients seen less than three to five sessions per week and, quite frankly, never thought to ask.

Like Freud, the analysts who adopted this policy believed that it furthered the treatment in several ways. It discouraged the patient from missing sessions to avoid exploring difficult issues. A therapist who chose not to hold the patient responsible for every missed session would inhabit the role of the good breast/mother, gratifying the patient's longing for a consistently giving, generous, maternal relationship. Such gratification would make understanding, analyzing, and resolving this longing significantly more difficult. In addition, deciding whether to charge for an absence was "playing God." Who is the therapist to decide whether a given absence warrants waiver of the fee? What standard would be used? And, regardless of the standard, the decision would ultimately be arbitrary. In addition, since charging for every missed session, regardless of the reason for the patient's absence, powerfully underscores the professional nature of the relationship, some therapists were concerned that not charging for all missed sessions would have a negative impact on the patient's experience of a personal-professional balance.

I knew some analysts who had developed different policies. My office colleague, Paul Chodoff, who had moved away from "classical analysis," thought that not differentiating missed from attended sessions was unethical because it deceived the insurance company, even if the company did not require this distinction. While I never understood how he made decisions regarding missed sessions, he disagreed strongly with charging for each session, regardless of circumstance. Several years into my analytic candidacy, my mother-in-law, who lived several hours away, died suddenly. My wife's analyst chose to bill her for every day of her absence, including the actual date of the funeral. My analyst did not charge me for the week that I was away. That experience rudely jolted me into a thorough reconsideration of my policy of charging for all missed sessions. I would add that personal experiences such as this have often led to a new perspective on my psychoanalytic work.

Although I had difficulty bringing it into focus, something about this policy had always troubled me. What I came to understand was that some causes for a patient's absence were such that I simply did not feel comfortable earning money from them on that day, a reaction reflecting that my relationship with patients was consistently both professional and personal. After a patient and I have decided to work together, I introduce the topic of missed appointments by saying something like: "I will hold you responsible for all missed appointments except for those situations when I prefer not to earn money because of the nature of the event that has resulted in your absence. Whenever you do not attend a session, if I can schedule another patient at that time or need to use it for a personal matter, there will be no charge."

To be sure, this policy is certainly arbitrary, but, regardless of the rationale, deciding to charge for all missed sessions is equally arbitrary. Such a policy may be clear, straightforward and entirely predictable. While applying it consistently may create the illusion that one is not choosing whether to charge or not, in point of fact, every application of the principle is a distinct decision. I apply the very same policy with all patients I see on a regular basis, regardless of frequency. I do not see why someone I see once a week should be treated differently from someone I see five times per week. I rent my time to each of them. Applying the same principle to everyone is also consistent with my not drawing a bright line between psychoanalytic psychotherapy and psychoanalysis.

Soon after I developed this policy, I was confronted with its consequences. I was about to begin an analysis with a woman who worked for the World Bank and was routinely out of the country for up to a month. She thought it "unfair" that she should have to pay for sessions she would miss through "no fault of my own," yet she wanted to resume meeting at the same early morning time when she returned. For me, while it was unfortunate that her profession created frequent, extended interruptions that would have a negative impact on our work, there was no avoiding the problem that my financial needs and her professional obligations were in direct conflict. While it seemed that she "would be paying for nothing," her expenditure insured that the hours we met would be reserved for her when she returned from her trips abroad. Since she very much valued not having our meetings interfere with her work schedule, she chose to pay for missed sessions and, while her reactions to my policy remained intense, our work continued productively.

I was working on this book in the midst of the COVID-19 pandemic and had spent many hours working by phone. (Because I feel compelled to look at the screen in an online conversation, I prefer talking on the phone.) Although I had worked by phone with several patients who moved prior to completing their therapy, when patients were unable to meet with me in person, we generally did not speak until they could return to my office. I believed that therapy had to be an "in-person" experience, an embodied conversation. Having learned that talking with patients on the phone can be very productive, if confronted with the same situation today I would certainly offer the option to talk with her while she was away. My experience during COVID has not altered my conviction that talking with patients in my office is considerably more impactful than talking with them on the phone or via video and that the time spent in transit to and from my office is time very well spent for me and my patients.

My policy regarding missed appointments highlights the constant, blunt impact of the arbitrary: "You didn't charge me when Jimmy was in the emergency room after being struck by a car but you did when he was at home with a strep throat and a high fever."

Each therapist needs to develop a policy that is not infused with defensiveness or guilt and that can be applied consistently. Inflexible (I charge for all missed sessions) or infinitely flexible, the policy is personal, individual, and arbitrary.

For me, one policy is non-negotiable. If an insurance company asks that missed sessions be identified on the invoice, failure to do so would be unethical and would corrupt the therapy. Since insurance companies are fully aware that many practitioners charge for missed sessions, if they do not specify that missed sessions be identified, I do not believe that the therapist is ethically required to differentiate between attended and unattended sessions.

◇◇◇◇◇◇◇◇◇◇◇◇◇◇◇◇◇◇◇◇◇◇◇◇◇◇◇◇◇◇◇◇◇

PSYCHOTHERAPY IS LIKE AN ANTIBIOTIC: ONE CHOOSES TYPE AND DOSAGE.

Although developing a plan of treatment is most effective when it emerges organically and is mutually created, psychiatrists and psychotherapists need to remain clear and unapologetic about owning and drawing upon their expertise.

This expertise does not involve knowing best how a patient should live their life, but it does grow out of each professional's education and experience. It is also helpful in reaching a diagnosis, knowing what treatment—psychological, pharmacological, or both—is best for which disorder, and determining which dosage of each therapeutic element will be most effective for a given individual—inpatient or outpatient, supportive, psychoanalytic, cognitive behavioral, or specialized treatments for conditions such as eating disorders, borderline personality disorders, and substance abuse are among the many types of therapies available. Every therapist has the responsibility to know the indications and contraindications for each.

Although it may seem obvious, it is worth emphasizing that the psychiatrist's or psychotherapist's education and professional experience will determine the treatment(s) and dosages that they are likely to recommend. A psychiatrist who has trained in a residency program that devotes limited didactic time to psychotherapy and provides little experience in a range of psychotherapies will have limited ability to determine the proper type of therapeutic treatment for their patients. If their program emphasizes a particular school of psychotherapeutic thought, other types of psychotherapies may be implicitly devalued.

If they have never been immersed in their own psychotherapy, a psychiatrist may devalue the importance and efficacy of psychotherapy and prescribe pharmacotherapy alone. Even if they do understand and appreciate the importance of psychotherapy, it is likely that they have never met with a patient more than once per week, and never met with patients for a number of years. Understandably they are likely to have drawn the conclusion that a once/week dosage of psychotherapy is indicated for most patients and a lower dose may well be adequate for many.

In a thoughtful, courageous book, David Carlat (2010) explores his psychiatric education and training at Massachusetts General Hospital. He consulted with a 40-year-old woman who was feeling discouraged, anxious, and hopeless. After 50 minutes, he had arrived at the conclusion that she was suffering from a major depressive disorder and recommended a serotonergic medication. He went on to say: "I did not tell Linda that psychotherapy might work just as well as medication for her, and that I had decided on medication because I received little training in therapy during my three years of psychiatric residency. Like many psychiatrists, I DON'T do psychotherapy because I CAN'T do psychotherapy." As I have discussed earlier, Dr. Carlat was practicing poor psychotherapy, and his self-examination and honesty enlighten us about the current state of psychotherapy training for psychiatrists in many psychiatric residencies.

When recommending a specific type of psychotherapy or a frequency of psychoanalytic sessions, I try to be very clear how my thinking has evolved from what the patient has shared with me. I have often been consulted by patients with multiple short-term psychotherapeutic experiences, yet they continue to suffer and have not achieved relief from their unhappiness. If the consultation provides therapist and patient with an understanding that unconscious motivations and long-held ways of adapting are countering the patient's desire for and ability to change, then both will understand that an intensive, relatively unstructured psychotherapy will be more likely to facilitate the desired goals of treatment. Similarly, if a patient with serious obsessive-compulsive difficulties has received little benefit from a psychoanalytic therapy, a recommendation for cognitive behavioral psychotherapy will be readily understood.

<><><><><><><><><><><><><><><><><><><><><><><><><>

THE "FUNDAMENTAL RULE" IS AN UNFORTUNATE CONCEPT.

In 1916, Freud introduced the concept of the "fundamental rule" which stipulated that the patient had to express, as best they could, anything that came to mind, without censorship or editing. The motivation for this instruction was logical and understandable. Fluidity of expression facilitates emergence of unconscious elements of the patient's mind and enables enduring transformation. Inevitably, when something important to the patient is deeply infused with shame, guilt, or anxiety, they will balk at sharing it with the therapist.

The fundamental rule was formulated to neutralize the patient's natural inclination to keep any number of things private from the therapist, and, of course, from themselves as well. In an exploration of the "fundamental rule" (Joseph 1990), I recommended that the clinical consultation should ideally lead to an understanding between therapist and patient of the role that unconscious thoughts, emotions, and motivations play in their distress and the rationale for the patient's speaking freely, without editing or censoring. If that understanding can be achieved, the importance of free association in creating a successful psychotherapeutic experience will be shared. When both patient and therapist hold this belief, saying whatever comes to mind will not be a rule imposed by an authority, a rule that may be submitted to willingly or grudgingly or rebelled against silently and sometimes unconsciously.

Most often the therapist will need to introduce the concept of free association and explain why it will facilitate the work and enable change. When free association is based on a shared understanding of its purpose and a commitment from patient to try to speak in this way, their inevitable reluctance or refusal to voice what they are thinking or feeling can be more readily explored. There is a profound, meaningful difference between: "I expect you to say everything that comes to mind" and "Our work together will be most productive if you give voice, as best you can, to everything that comes to mind."

For patients who meet with me once or twice per week, I say that the therapy will be most productive if they speak about whatever is important to them, a slightly different but not insignificant phrase. Although the desirability of associating freely has been understood and agreed to, patients often express bitter resentment when they feel required to say everything that comes to mind, even though we have a shared understanding of its benefit. When the patient feels that they "have to" say everything that is on their mind, they have created the experience of a controlling and dominating therapist. This reaction can be more productively explored when free association has been a shared goal, not a rule promulgated by an expert and imposed by an authority. Running up against their own powerful reluctance to speak freely is the most compelling evidence of a patient's "resistance."

There are many meaningful psychotherapies such as brief psychotherapy, family therapy, and cognitive-behavioral psychotherapy in which it is not desirable for the patient to say everything that comes to mind. In addition, for some patients, associating freely is harmful, flooding them with intense feelings and deeply unsettling thoughts that disrupt their thinking and functioning. For many patients, however, attempting to speak to the therapist in the manner of free association is powerfully transformative and is a most effective way to achieve lasting change.

When a patient gives voice to thoughts and feelings without editing, the analyst's ability to listen psychoanalytically, to listen with "evenly hovering attention" (Freud 1912), is facilitated. When the patient listens to and understands how the analyst has achieved understanding of a matter that had seemed inexplicable, their ability to speak freely is facilitated. In an ongoing psychoanalytic conversation, with frequent meetings over a long period of time, the ability of each party to successfully accomplish this aspect of their job is strengthened.

<><><><><><><><><><><><><><><><><><><><><><><><>

THE PSYCHOTHERAPEUTIC RELATIONSHIP IS NOT A MODEL FOR ANY OTHER RELATIONSHIP.

It is profoundly ironic that a relationship which is deeply meaningful, fosters significant learning, and facilitates the transformation of one's self is not a model for any other kind of relationship. It is equally ironic that the very quality of its uniqueness enables psychoanalytic therapy to be effective and enables patients to improve their relationships with others. Patient and analyst meet frequently, in a completely private space, with the therapist, but not the patient, ethically committed to absolute confidentiality. In no other relationship is it helpful for one person to try to convey whatever they are experiencing in the moment, and for the other person to listen respectfully and empathically, to clarify the causes of suffering, and to respond compassionately.

Throughout a psychoanalytic psychotherapy the patient is continually assessing how consistently the therapist can adhere to the commitment that total openness will be responded to empathically and with a goal of furthering understanding and change. The patient may express insults, seductiveness, anger, competitiveness, contempt, stone-cold fury, shame, deep sorrow, lust, and intense love, always accompanied by an ever-present, if not always conscious, concern that the therapist will respond hurtfully. If a therapy is to be productive, every therapist will, at times, be profoundly unsettled and wounded by the patient's words and behavior.

Some patients experience immediate, deep trust in the therapist, but most are initially cautious, wary of being embarrassed, mis-understood, shamed, denigrated, exploited or seduced. One can only have enduring confidence in trust that has been earned over a meaningful period of time, trust that has been repeatedly and seriously tested.

Patients who rapidly develop such trust have an intense hunger for a completely safe, infinitely trusting relationship, and that desire leads them to experience it at the outset of treatment. Only after the therapy has deepened can they begin to doubt and be wary of their therapist. Some patients may trust the therapist "completely" to counterbalance their unconscious, unsettling sense of vulnerability and profound distrust. Patients who have no apparent concern about being hurt when they allow themselves to be vulnerable may also be reflecting a hidden concern that they do not trust themselves, that they harbor cruel, sadistic desires that terrify them.

Although severe trauma in adulthood can engender mistrust or suspicion, these states of mind most often stem from childhood experience. Since psychoanalysis is structured to make developmentally early aspects of the self powerfully active and accessible within the therapeutic relationship, both patient and therapist experience the intensities and vulnerabilities that are central aspects of childhood. The emergence of hidden longings, emotions, and painful experiences from childhood contribute to the patient's experience that the relationship with the therapist is one-sided. Only patients make themselves vulnerable. While sexual exploitation receives the most intense scrutiny by the public and the profession, other, more subtle, harmful exploitations may occur. A therapist's voyeurism, narcissism, and unconscious desire to avoid certain topics may be hidden, but their impact will shape the therapy and be hurtful to the patient.

A woman in her 30s had been in psychoanalysis five times a week for a number of years and, since both patient and analyst agreed that they were stuck, she was referred to me for a consultation. Midway through our first meeting, I experienced the thought that it was important that I explore the subject of sex. I had no idea what stimulated that conviction, and I sat quietly with it for awhile. I would add that the experience of something being unconsciously communicated is common when one listens psychoanalytically. As we continued to talk, I remained convinced that issues around sexuality were contributing to the impasse in her analysis. I gently inquired whether she and her analyst had talked about sex. I do not know who experienced greater surprise, the patient by my question or myself by her reply. In many years of analytic work, she had never volunteered anything relating to sex, and her analyst had never observed and wondered about its absence. I said to the patient that both she and her analyst were avoiding the topic of sexuality, which I believed must be an important contributor to her distress and to the "stuckness" that she and her analyst experienced. I also encouraged her to relay my words directly and explicitly to her analyst.

Several years later, after her analyst had retired, the patient returned to see me. She told me that she had not informed her analyst about my observations and, in the several years they continued to work together, the impact of my consultation was never explored. She and I worked together for many years, beginning with a shared understanding that we would not avoid discussing sexuality. While progress was anything but easy, over time she gradually and painfully shared with me that she had been tormented by a number of sexual concerns and experiences. This dramatic experience highlights the ways in which the therapist's unconscious and sometimes deliberate avoidance can collude with the patient's vulnerability to the detriment of both; the patient's desire for change and the therapist's desire to provide the most help to the patient will be thwarted by their mutual avoidance.

After practicing psychoanalysis for many years, I realized that it was sometimes useful to clarify with patients that the psychoanalytic relationship is not a model for any other relationship—not with a spouse, parent, children, psychotherapeutic supervisor, or anyone else. In every other relationship, we must decide whether it will further or harm the relationship to share what is on our mind with that person. The uniqueness of the therapeutic relationship is an essential factor that facilitates the patient's profound attachment to the therapist. And, since the therapist is known only within the psychotherapeutic relationship, patients are understandably prone to believe that the therapist acts the same in their other relationships.

The psychotherapeutic relationship is anchored in mutuality, but its mutuality is idiosyncratic. I believe that, for the most part, it is not in the interest of the therapy for a therapist to speak directly about their own pain, their own vulnerabilities, or their own shameful experiences. Such disclosures are the task of the patient. Although this may be well understood by the patient, the vulnerability inherent in self-disclosure is often reflected in their bitter complaints that the therapist does not share their own conflicts and anxieties. The therapist asks that the patient try to fulfill the role of being a patient, that they attempt to speak with complete candor and be whoever they are in the moment. That is a tall order, indeed, and frequently results in the patient acting in nasty, stubborn withholding ways. But the ask from the therapist to continually fulfill the role of therapist is also difficult, a task they inevitably will sometimes fail to fulfill. These two "asks" comprise the foundation of the mutuality of psychotherapy.

At the beginning of therapy, patient and therapist understand that, if meaningful enduring change has been achieved, they will agree that ending the relationship is desirable. This is another unique, ironic aspect of the clinical therapeutic relationship. Such a mutual understanding is essential to the efficacy of any psychotherapy, based on the premise that when the intensities of the patient's many transference reactions have been "worked through" (they cannot be eliminated), and their sense of themselves has been meaningfully transformed, the work of the therapy has been done well enough and a time to end the therapy should be determined. Sometimes patient and therapist continue to work together primarily to postpone saying goodbye. In addition to avoiding the experience of mourning, patient and therapist may also extend the therapy so that they do not have to accept the inevitable disappointments that grow from hopes not fully realized and changes not accomplished.

After a psychotherapeutic relationship ends, the patient and therapist will not have any further psychotherapeutic conversations. The end of therapy does not mean that the patient will stop developing greater self-understanding and achieving further growth, nor will they cease to experience an analytic relationship with their therapist. As Lear (2004) has noted, the analysis ends but its therapeutic action does not. Quite commonly, patients discover much about themselves after the analysis has ended, precisely because they are not meeting with their analyst and do not experience the immediacy of their transference anxieties and vulnerabilities.

Changes that occur after ending treatment can, somewhat paradoxically, enable the discovery of aspects of themselves that had remained hidden or not fully integrated. Therapists, too, may gain greater understanding of their patients and their own countertransference reactions after the therapy has ended. Although the professional aspect of the relationship no longer develops, the patient will always continue to experience their analyst as their analyst. While it is helpful to conceptualize personal and professional aspects of the therapeutic relationship, there is only one, indivisible relationship, just as there is only one, indivisible self.

In my experience, patients and therapists have a range of relationships following the end of psychotherapy. Some have no contact whatsoever, no holiday cards, letters about changes in their lives, no calls to resume treatment. In psychoanalytic institutes, patients and analysts often have frequent interactions ranging from working on committees to having a much more personal relationship, including dining at each other's homes. I believe it is essential that the patient be the one to initiate any relationship that will develop after the psychotherapy, and that a significant period of time should elapse before there is any contact. This period facilitates meaningful grieving and the waning of the transferential aspects of the relationship. I will explore this topic in greater detail in a section devoted to retirement.

◇◇◇◇◇◇◇◇◇◇◇◇◇◇◇◇◇◇◇◇◇◇◇◇◇◇◇◇◇◇◇◇◇◇◇

EVERYTHING LEARNED IN PSYCHOTHERAPY IS RELEVANT TO ONE'S OTHER IMPORTANT RELATIONSHIPS. EVERYTHING THAT HAS BEEN ACTIVE IN ONE'S IMPORTANT RELATIONSHIPS WILL BE REFLECTED IN THEIR PSYCHOTHERAPY.

A man in his 50s sought treatment because, since adolescence, he had experienced difficult conflicts with authority figures. For several years of intensive treatment, we explored a number of important issues, including extensive discussion of his difficult relationships with authority figures, including, not surprisingly, his father. These conversations contributed to significant changes in his professional and personal relationships, and the patient frequently expressed satisfaction that I had helped him to change in meaningful ways. He rarely was late, paid each bill promptly, appeared to speak freely, and was rarely unhappy with me, even when I regularly took a month's vacation in August. It was all too easy for me to bask in the glow of our accomplishments and disregard the premise that I felt was relevant to any psychotherapy.

At some point, I became aware that I was ignoring my own aphorism and noted to the patient that his conflicts with authority had never seemed alive in our relationship. After a long pause, he told me that he had been quite critical that I seemed so very private and acknowledged that he often wanted to make fun of my being short and mock me for always wearing a necktie. In the ensuing months, he gradually became aware of his deep resentment at "having to meet" with me so frequently and having paid me so much money over the years.

In the ensuing months, he began to derive more satisfaction from his professional relationships and noted that he did not have to be as vigilant about his desire to challenge authority. His relationships with his wife and family also became less based on his being the authority figure at home. Had I not "remembered" this aphorism, I seriously doubt that the authority struggles he waged with me would ever have surfaced, or that his relationship with authority—others' and his own—would have changed as much.

Keeping this principle in mind makes it much more likely that the therapist will be aware that certain, highly charged issues are being "excluded" from their relationship with the patient and their psychotherapeutic work. Three of the many common therapeutic experiences include the patient who is never dissatisfied with the analyst despite a life replete with bitter disappointment, the patient with a bad temper but who never gets angry with the therapist, and the patient who frequently falls quickly in love with others but is unaware of loving the therapist. The principle also reinforces the knowledge that, when the conflicts are alive in the consulting room, enduring change and personal growth are facilitated.

◇◇◇◇◇◇◇◇◇◇◇◇◇◇◇◇◇◇◇◇◇◇◇◇◇◇◇◇◇◇◇◇◇◇

THE UNKNOWN THERAPIST IS AN ILLUSION.

An oft-heard lament from patients, sometimes expressed with disappointment, sometimes with bitterness, mournfully proclaims that they do not know "anything" about us, whereas they have shared so much of themselves with us and so often made themselves vulnerable. Such unhappiness may reflect the patient's having been raised in a family in which the parents did not want to be known and in which secrets silently perfused and distorted their familial relationships and sense of themselves. If a patient never expresses intense curiosity about us, its absence is significant and warrants exploration. The absence might reflect a powerful, unconscious longing to know us deeply, intense sexual curiosity, or other desires associated with painful embarrassment and shame. The seeming absence of any curiosity about us may also protect the patient from experiencing the disappointment and resentment inherent in the fact that we generally find it preferable to keep many aspects of ourselves private.

Although "I don't know anything about you" is a frequent protest, patients actually know us extremely well. They come to know us through the ways in which we interact with them including our consistency, emotional expressiveness, sense of humor (or lack of it), and responsiveness to their thoughts and emotions. They come to know us through the ways in which we have come to know and understand them, by our insightfulness and our empathy but also by our blind spots and vulnerabilities. Ironically, some patients who express a desire to know us better are surprisingly unsettled by the impact of coming to know us and the intimacy that has nurtured such knowing.

The different roles and tasks of patient and therapist shape the asymmetry of the psychotherapeutic relationship, but this aspect of the relationship does not preclude their coming to know us and know us very well, albeit only within the psychoanalytic relationship, with all its unique characteristics and constraints. The unhappiness at not knowing us better also reflects a powerful desire to be involved fully with us. A patient who, with great sincerity, laments that they "do not know us," is giving expression to the deep sorrow created by the limits of the relationship.

Therapists who have had their own meaningful psychotherapy have experienced the impact of the unique relationship between patient and therapist. Therapists who have not can only try to take it on faith and faith, unfortunately, can only take the therapist so far. Analytic candidates are required to have a personal analysis to help them become aware of and gain respect for the depth and breadth of their unconscious mind, as well as its vulnerabilities, desires, memories, and blind spots. This experience also demonstrates the breathtaking power of psychotherapy to shape their relationship with their analyst and other important persons in their life, as well as their sense of self. Their experience as a patient also engenders understanding and respect for the difficulty of being a patient and compassion when their analysis is blunted by their "resistance," be it conscious withholding or unconscious avoidance. These experiences are unknown to therapists who have never had their own psychotherapy, and, in my opinion, this limits their effectiveness.

Being in analysis during one's training facilitates the exploration of blind spots and countertransference reactions that are regularly reflected in clinical practice. If productive, a therapist's personal psychoanalysis also creates a deep conviction of the power of psychoanalysis. This conviction, which has been earned in their personal psychotherapeutic trench, helps sustain every therapist when the work with a patient seems hopeless.

THE CONCEPT OF SELF-DISCLOSURE IS MISLEADING.

"How did you break your arm?" asks one patient. "Three months is a long time to be away; is everything OK?" asks another when you inform him of a prolonged absence for upcoming cardiac surgery. To answer an inquiry about how one's arm broke, to inform a patient that one is going to have bypass surgery, these and myriad questions about one's absence, background, family, etc., constitute what is generally understood to comprise the broad field of "self-disclosure." The term implies that, absent sharing such specific information, central aspects of one's self are not disclosed in every interaction with every patient.

Given that our personal selves are at the center of our professional selves, every component of ourselves, especially when working with patients intensively, is relentlessly buffeted and challenged by multiple transference and countertransference reactions. Our personal selves are integral to every moment of every psychotherapy, always hiding in plain sight. To "forget" that one's self is always known, to some degree, by the patient may give respite from this pervasive tension, but the respite is an illusion.

Perhaps the most detrimental impact of this illusion is that, when therapists consciously choose to share something personal (e.g., how I broke my arm; where I went on vacation; whether I saw a certain movie or have read a certain book), they may feel that they have done something wrong, or have transgressed the sacrosanct rules of abstinence and anonymity. When questioned about whether he had seen a certain movie or read a particular book, one of my most helpful supervisors always answered, "I am interested in the movie you saw." For many years I never questioned his advice, but I have come to hold the conviction that, if I have seen the movie (or read the book, or been to Rome, etc.), I cannot help but listen differently to what the patient tells me about its meaning and impact on them, and my responses will be significantly different than if I had not seen it. From the perspective of self-disclosure, even if I provide no explicit indication whether I have seen the movie, in the course of the discussion I will wordlessly inform the patient whether I have seen it. I now believe the far better choice is to answer the question and then explore the patient's response to the movie and their reaction to the fact that I have seen it, too. Patients and I often have significantly different responses to a book or movie, differences that, when explored, lead to very productive work. Furthermore, patients who have significant conflict about their own curiosity and the risks it entails (curiosity killed the cat), are very likely to be unconsciously aware of their therapist's aversion to this kind of sharing, with the unfortunate consequence that the conflicts surrounding curiosity may not receive the attention they deserve.

Many years before the internet, one of my supervisors unhesitatingly answered any question if the information was in the public record, and I have often wondered how he would have reacted to the age of the internet. Some therapists, after an initial meeting, urge patients not to search for information about them, and patients frequently feel guilty about Googling their therapists, as much because of their excitement as for having transgressed an absolute rule. Although the boundaries of privacy have been greatly extended, I believe that whatever a patient might learn about me via internet research will not have a negative impact on the therapy.

"Anonymity" and "abstinence" do not refer to this kind of information. Rather, as discussed previously, they reflect the understanding that the therapist has a responsibility not to burden the patient with information about their private life, conflicts, moods, vulnerabilities, and concerns. To do so might silently influence the patient to take care of them by avoiding being critical, nasty or scornful or by being especially solicitous and nurturing.

Long before the internet exponentially expanded the boundaries of privacy, patients became aware of aspects of their therapist's life, even in large, metropolitan cities. Marriage and divorce; the birth, marriage, and death of children; illness; and an endless list of "private" information often became known with little or no research by the patient, whatsoever. By happenstance, patients often learn a great deal about their therapist. Does he play tennis and, if so, is he a good sport? Does she subscribe to the symphony, give good parties, drink too much, or have a bad temper? In my opinion, to introduce such information into therapy is rarely useful, but only when a therapist feels threatened by information the patient has or might learn does it have a negative impact. A therapist may well feel intruded upon when certain "external facts" are discovered, but, if they are not overly unsettled by what the patient has discovered, the therapeutic relationship may actually be strengthened.

◇◇◇

EVERY PATIENT HOPES TO KNOW THEMSELVES MORE FULLY, TO BE KNOWN BY ANOTHER, AND TO KNOW THEIR THERAPIST.

It bears repeating that psychoanalytic psychotherapy is structured to facilitate the discovery and expression of unconscious desires, emotions, thoughts, and memories in order to facilitate a deeper understanding of one's self and others and to enable meaningful personal growth. Each of us carries powerful desires to be known and understood by a caring "other," desires that, to one degree or another, have been both met and unsatisfied by caregivers throughout our lives. It is no wonder, then, that our patients, like each of us, having experienced multiple disappointments, sometimes bitter and profoundly damaging, find themselves caring deeply about us and wanting to know us well.

Fear and shame about the intensity of these desires and the fantasies associated with them are sometimes reflected by a seemingly total lack of interest in the therapist, little apparent reaction to our absences, and, not infrequently, resentment if we should express any interest or see value in reflecting upon the therapeutic relationship. Several patients with intense concern about "boundaries" told me firmly at the outset of our work that they did not want to know anything about me. Patients who fear knowing their analyst also dread coming to know themselves.

The very nature of the analytic relationship engenders deep, often quiet, pain that is rooted in the ways the relationship is restricted. The patient experiences us as being consistently attentive, concerned, and helpful, but only during scheduled times. While the desire for a personal relationship with the analyst—as friend, companion, competitor, enemy, or lover—reflects the suffering, jealousy, and resentment at being excluded from the parental couple and other aspects of familial relationships, it is also rooted in the very nature of psychoanalytic treatment. Ironically, the better patients and therapist learn to work together and the more successfully the therapy assists patients to know, accept, respect, and transform themselves, the greater the frustrations about the clearly defined, consistently maintained limits of the analytic relationship.

In my psychoanalytic training, I was cautioned against "gratifying the patient's transference wishes," as though patients do not always have multiple, concurrent transference reactions, some of which I might be gratifying while simultaneously frustrating others. The analyst, however, ought not attempt to frustrate the patient. Rather, their adherence to the structure and limits of psychoanalytic psychotherapy facilitates awareness and gradual waning of unfulfilled and unfulfillable wishes and desires rooted in childhood. A therapist who presents a "blank screen" to the patient will engender a reaction to a distant, private individual, and fears of gratifying the patient's transference wishes may lead the therapist to be unnecessarily withholding.

I strongly believe that an important aspect of productive psychotherapy includes my being able and willing to explain, as best I can, how I have arrived at a certain hypothesis or emotional reaction, and what I believe has allowed me to experience the patient's unexpressed and often unconscious thoughts and feelings. Patients do not routinely inquire about my thinking, and most often, I think it preferable not to disrupt the flow of the conversation by introducing it. However, I am always prepared to share whatever understanding I am aware of, even if the best I can do is to say, "I have had a persistent, strong hunch...."

If a patient asks, "What led you to think that?" I think it better to provide the best answer I can. The Oracle at Delphi is a poor model for a psychoanalytic psychotherapist. It encourages a particular kind of dependency in which the patient forsakes confidence in and underestimates the potential of his own mind in the psychoanalytic work. Explaining how we have arrived at an understanding of the patient is frequently difficult. Sometimes our "knowing" is uncanny. Regardless, being open to sharing how our mind has worked has a powerful impact on the therapeutic relationship and furthers the patient's ability to change in the way they wish.

I was taught that answering personal questions would interfere with exploration of the patient's fantasies, but, in fact, answering one question always leads to additional questions and generates new fantasies. Knowing where I live will be consistent or inconsistent with the patient's fantasy, but that knowledge only stimulates new fantasies such as the size and cost of the house, how long I have lived there, how it is decorated and on and on. A slavish insistence on privacy may reflect a therapist's personal character more than the implementation of a useful aspect of psychoanalytic technique. I often argued with a very good friend whose analytic work I respected deeply about whether we had "dialogues" with our patients. He insistently balked at that concept, reflecting the fact that he was, in all aspects of his life, a very private person. Deciding that, in principle, one should never share personal information with the patient spares one from repeatedly wrestling with whether it is better to share or not to share.

<><><><><><><><><><><><><><><><><><><><><><><><><><>

EVERY THERAPIST HAS A "PERSONAL SELF" AND A "PROFESSIONAL SELF."

Clinicians reshape and refine their psychotherapeutic selves over the lifetime of their career. I have worked in many professional settings, fulfilled a number of professional roles, and have had the privilege of teaching, supervising, and being an administrator for medical students, hospital staff, psychiatric residents, analytic candidates, graduate therapists, and psychoanalysts. I have also treated patients in hospitals, community mental health centers, and in my private practice. These diverse experiences and my medical, psychiatric, and psychoanalytic education are reflected in what I think of as my "professional self."

My professional self reflects all the aspects of my professional knowledge, personality traits, temperament, and experience that are central to Dr. Joseph, physician, psychiatrist and psychoanalyst. Somewhat unexpectedly, the very process of writing this book has generated a much richer and more nuanced understanding of what I refer to as my "personal self" and has clarified how that self is inextricably interwoven with my professional self.

I want to emphasize again that I have only one self, and that the self is unitary. The self is like white light that, when a prism is shifted, is seen to be comprised of many wavelengths. Each self has many aspects, one being predominant in a given situation. So, too, with emotions. Shift the prism of anger and the wavelengths of annoyance, irritation, resentment, anger, fury, or murderous rage will become visible. So, also, with the emotions of love, sorrow, guilt, and all others. When I speak of a personal and professional self, each is comprised of many, distinct qualities.

I was David Joseph for 26 years before I became Dr. Joseph. I have had two psychoanalyses, the first when I was in medical school, the second when I was learning to be a psychoanalyst. Both my analysts helped me to know myself better and to grow in significant and much desired if often painful ways. The person who needed and benefited greatly from these analytic experiences, the self that I brought to my psychiatric and psychoanalytic education, is what I conceptualize as my personal self and is at the very center of my medical self, my psychiatric self, and my psychoanalytic self. All that I have learned in medical school, psychiatric residency, psychoanalytic institute and throughout my career has been absorbed by that person, that self. I would not have it any other way, but, more importantly, it would have been impossible for me to have it any other way.

Psychoanalytic educators have principles, technical interventions, and strategies that can be defined, elaborated, and taught. We can describe certain actions that facilitate the patient's sense of safety, allowing them to feel less vulnerable as they relate their stories, give voice to their sorrow, rage, sexual desire, and love. We can instruct our students how best to end an hour, when to introduce administrative matters such as absences or fee increases, ways of conceptualizing dreams, and the principles of exploring the adaptive (defense) mechanisms that one uses when feeling vulnerable. But the techniques we teach are more like those taught to aspiring writers, painters, and musicians than those taught to surgeons.

Unlike surgical techniques, psychoanalytic techniques are dramatically transformed when they are moved from the classroom to the consulting room. The person who absorbs, metabolizes, and incorporates their knowledge will profoundly shape how it is utilized. This personal self is at the center of every psychoanalytic self. That is a major reason why my two analyses were so very different. My two analysts, in addition to having different theoretical orientations, were very different people. And to be sure, I had changed in significant ways in the years between my two analyses. This is one of the essential dualities of being a psychoanalyst: personal self and professional self, David Joseph and Dr. Joseph.

In the closing lines of "Among School Children," William Butler Yeats has evocatively expressed this duality:

O chestnut tree, great rooted blossomer,
Are you the leaf, the blossom or the bole?
O body swayed to music, O brightening glance
How can we know the dancer from the dance?

If we are not careful, our teaching of psychotherapeutic techniques may implicitly ask that the psychotherapist try to separate their unique personality, temperament, and character from their psychotherapeutic practice. Such an effort, in addition to engendering the frustration inherent when attempting the impossible, can suggest the desirability of a psychotherapeutic relationship in which the therapist tries to be "impersonal" and emotionally blanketed.

Early in my career, I learned that a well-known analyst never removed his sport coat because he believed that to do so would be acting seductively. Another proudly informed his audience that, over a long career, no patient ever knew where he went on vacation. A therapist who tries to adhere too closely, too literally, to any method will elicit transference reactions to someone who has constrained the expression of their individuality. While such reactions can be usefully explored, their centrality may be misunderstood as primarily rooted in the patient's prior relationships and not, to a significant degree, as a response to the therapist's attempting to adhere to an "ideal" psychoanalytic school of thought or method.

One corollary of the centrality of a personal self is reflected in the many, and to my mind, unfortunate efforts to define "analyzability." There are a number of disorders, especially in their acute phase, in which unstructured dialogue, and a quietly attentive therapist have a disorganizing impact on the patient. However, trying to determine, in the abstract, whether someone is "analyzable" treats the patient's condition as though it were a metastatic malignancy and asking whether medication is likely to be effective. When consulting with a patient, the most helpful question asks, "Is it likely that this person will have a productive psychotherapy with me or would they work better with another analyst or a therapist?" Learning that a patient has previously been in psychoanalysis conveys some meaningful information but does not provide any sense of the day-to-day experience of the patient during their analysis, does not indicate whether they will be able to work productively with you, whether you and this patient will be a "good fit."

◇◇◇◇◇◇◇◇◇◇◇◇◇◇◇◇◇◇◇◇◇◇◇◇◇◇◇◇◇◇◇◇◇◇◇

A THERAPIST'S WISH TO ASK A QUESTION REFLECTS THE PATIENT'S CONFLICTS.

Earlier, I mentioned an incident in my career regarding a colleague who was beginning his training analysis to become a psychoanalyst and was informed by his analyst that, after the consultation sessions had been completed, he would not answer any questions. That was many years ago, and I chalked up my difficulty understanding the rationale and value of such a stance to my fledgling psychoanalytic status. Questions, many experienced analysts taught, may be experienced as intrusive, subtly critical, and usually not effective in facilitating a wider, deeper exploration.

Several years into my psychoanalytic education, while attending a meeting of the American Psychoanalytic Association, I listened to a clinical case presentation of a patient who was six years into their analysis. The analyst discussing the case asked the presenter whether the patient had any siblings. The answer, "I don't know; the topic has never come up," left me stunned. At that time, I understood the analyst's stance to be grounded on the principle of free association—one waits for the patient spontaneously to raise important material. But even then, I began to doubt whether inquiring should be rigorously avoided. Now, some 45 years later, I continue to have respected colleagues who do not ask questions of their patients. All of this has provoked considerable thought about the dynamics of the analyst's questions, whether they are best kept private, asked in some disguised or disavowed way, or expressed as an explicit inquiry.

When a question arises in the therapist's mind, some process between patient and therapist has stimulated the formation of the inquiry. The material about which the therapist is interested may not have been consciously withheld, but any desire to inquire about unspoken material raises an important question: "Why has the patient not already provided the answer?" Consider the frame of mind a therapist might have in the following situations: "I had a big argument with my husband yesterday and went to the movies by myself. It was a terrific movie...." Or "I spend too much time watching pornography. I wish I could develop other things to interest me when I am alone."

In the first instance, the therapist is likely to note that the patient provided no specifics about the fight or what state of mind they hoped to dissipate by going to the movies. In the second situation, the therapist may understand that the patient feels ashamed and embarrassed not only by the amount of time they spend watching pornography, but also by the specifics of the sexually explicit films they prefer and by their masturbation fantasies. In both situations, the patient has stimulated the therapist's wish to inquire, and the therapist must decide how to intervene in a manner that will reduce the patient's sense of vulnerability and deepen the discussion.

I have come to understand that my desire to ask a question, especially when the desire is very powerful, is indicative of the patient having engendered in me a burning wish to inquire about something while simultaneously, sometimes desperately, wanting to keep that material private. Unconsciously feeling intense anxiety and vulnerability, they have not given expression to important information. The more intense my desire to ask a question, the more vulnerable I assume the patient to be, and the more tactful my actions must be. In such situations, I might well elect to ask nothing and wait until our work has reduced the patient's sense of vulnerability so that they will bring it into our work. If that does not occur, I will have a greater understanding of the patient's sensitivity and will be better able to frame my inquiry in a less threatening manner.

In an article that I have reread many times, Jacob Arlow (1995) argues persuasively that analysts should be wary of developing a style which he describes as "stilted listening." A corollary recommendation, implied by the title, is that therapists be mindful that one can easily develop a style of "stilted speaking." A vigilant determination to avoid asking questions can easily contribute to a stiff, restricted psychotherapeutic conversation. It can also lead to the therapist's misperception that they are not asking questions when, in fact, they are indirectly asking them all the time. "I'm not clear how you reached the decision to go to the movie," or "You are concerned about sharing with me the specific nature of the pornographic films you watch," are interventions that implicitly ask a question but do so in a manner that is less intrusive and less challenging.

As I noted at the outset of this discussion, when considering whether to ask a question, I privately wonder why the patient has not volunteered the information that seems quite important to me. Sometimes it feels more helpful to simply ask the question and subsequently explore the reasons the patient had not voluntarily shared the information. At other times, the better choice is to say, "We've been talking for a long time, and I'm struck that you haven't said anything about whether you have any siblings or are an only child."

SOME ASSOCIATIONS ARE SILENT.
SOME CONTENT IS ABSENT.

In reflecting further upon the instance in which the analyst, after years of working with the patient, did not know whether they had any siblings, I came to conceptualize this phenomenon as "absent content." I define absent content as an emotionally charged experience that the patient, feeling vulnerable in a deep, pervasive way, has completely avoided bringing into their psychotherapy, either consciously withheld or unconsciously barred from awareness.

In the case presentation in which there was no mention of siblings, one would not be shocked to learn that the patient had a sibling who died, and that their sadness, guilt, and shame over their pleasure in having one less rival led them to unconsciously eliminate siblings from their analysis. I can imagine that the analyst was simply adhering to the principle of free association, but it is also quite possible that, in this instance, the patient unconsciously and powerfully influenced the analyst not to ask about siblings, and that the analyst colluded with them, albeit by adhering strictly to respected analytic technique.

A patient may be deeply and meaningfully involved in therapy and never introduce the topic of sex. Or they may talk endlessly about their stressful relationship with their irascible, explosive father and fears of their own explosiveness, never mentioning their mother. Or the therapist may come to realize that they have no idea about the patient's religious upbringing or current practice.

Like instances in which the therapist has a burning desire to ask a question, absent content frequently reflects the patient's vulnerability and their fears of discovering and exploring hidden material with the therapist.

Sometimes, highly charged material will be shared early in treatment and then seems to disappear from the psychoanalytic field entirely. A woman told me early in her analysis, her voice quivering with fear and shame, that she had been sexually abused as a child. She did not provide details then, and I thought it preferable to let her tell me more when we knew each other better and she felt safer. Repeatedly, many months would go by, and I would suddenly realize that she never referred to her abuse. I would note this, she and I would have a meaningful but limited discussion about how painful it was for her to remember and discuss it with me, and then the topic would vanish again. Bringing this pattern to her attention allowed her to understand, in a visceral way, the pervasive sense of vulnerability, guilt, and shame that had haunted her forever. It was also a powerful demonstration of her ability to influence me to "forget" her traumatic childhood experience.

The silent association reflects a similar interaction between patient and therapist in which the therapist is certain that the patient has not mentioned something that they must be wrestling with. A remarkably common and surprising situation occurs when a pregnant therapist encounters a patient who, month after month, leading even into the third trimester, makes absolutely no mention about the changes in her body, much less react overtly to her pregnancy. Or a therapist may shave his beard or dye their hair and find that some patients act as though they have not observed anything different.

These "silent associations" may be the product of deliberate withholding but, surprisingly often, they reflect the absence of conscious perception. Like absent content, silent associations can be fruitfully understood by understanding that the patient has ignited in the therapist the strong desire to ask, "You haven't said anything about the fact that I have shaved my beard."

How long one waits and how best to address a silent association will depend on the specific situation, but for the therapist to avoid making it an object of analysis immobilizes patient and therapist in a therapeutic pas de deux that tries to dance around some central material. The therapist understands the patient's intense anxiety about commenting upon the change, and, by noting the silent association, takes the initiative that the patient has avoided. In so doing, they silently reassure the patient that they can tolerate and respect whatever response the patient provides.

A major sociocultural event that must have powerfully impacted both patient and therapist but is not addressed by the patient represents another category of absent content. The tragedies of 9/11 and the murder of George Floyd exemplify two intense, earth-shattering experiences that, if they were not addressed by the patient, deserve attention, with the initial intervention being to note their absence. Patients may believe that to speak about current events will be interpreted as avoidance, and some psychotherapists may share a similar perspective, but the psychotherapeutic relationship is not hermetically sealed, nor will it be contaminated by current events, including those much less dramatic. Rather, exploring important sociocultural matters enriches the therapy for both patient and therapist. It also reminds both patient and therapist of the profound impact of sociocultural experience in shaping ourselves, both currently and in the past.

Therapists themselves may be so powerfully impacted by some external public event that they know they cannot be fully present. I learned of the January 6, 2021 assault on the Capitol shortly before my final session of the day. Because of COVID-19, I was working from home, and I called my patient to say that I had just learned of the assault and was certain that I would not be able to listen to or speak with him in a meaningful way. I also told him that I regretted cancelling the appointment on such notice and would speak with him the following day.

In that meeting, the patient, who was studying to become a psychoanalyst, expressed shock at my decision. He believed that a psychoanalyst should be able to attend to their work, regardless of external circumstances—illness in himself or family being the only exceptions. Not surprisingly, this experience led to a very fruitful discussion.

OFFERING ADVICE TO SOMEONE WHO NEEDS IT DOES NOT MAKE ONE AN ADVICE COLUMNIST. OFFERING ADVICE TO SOMEONE WHO DOES NOT NEED IT IS HARMFUL.

Advice is "an opinion given or offered as to what action to take; counsel; recommendation" (OED). Although it may be taken as an explicit directive or experienced as merely suggestive, advice is not inherently about telling someone what to do. Advice implicitly states: "From my understanding of you and your situation, this is what I recommend you do."

As a physician, my medical and psychopharmacological knowledge may lead me to recommend, sometimes very strongly, that a patient choose to be hospitalized, go to the emergency room because they have acute GI bleeding, call their primary care physician, or take a certain psychiatric medication. Patients with a disorganized mental state whose thinking and judgment is disordered cannot exercise proper judgment and need the clinician to exercise judgment for them. Patients who are not psychotic may sometimes benefit from strongly worded advice.

When a therapist learns that a patient is about to engage in an action that would likely have disastrous repercussions, better first to recommend that they refrain from the action and then explore why they did not draw upon their better judgment. Were they trying to get the therapist to provide advice to reinforce their insistent belief in their own inadequacy, to worry or frighten the therapist?

Were they looking forward to rejecting the therapist's advice? All hypotheses can be productively explored after the advice has been given, regardless of whether the patient follows it.

The urge to give advice to a patient grows from the analyst's private thought, "If I were in your shoes I would most certainly...." When the therapist is positive that they would choose a different course of action than that contemplated by the patient, the therapist does not understand something essential about the patient's perception of the situation and the consequences of their contemplated action. A patient barraged me in our first meeting about how miserable he had been for each of his 25 years of marriage. So pervasive, long-standing, and painful was his unhappiness that I thought, with considerable conviction: "This man should get a divorce," which would have been hurtful to recommend since I had absolutely no understanding of why he had chosen to stay in a marriage that he felt was so dreadful.

Whenever I am strongly inclined to give advice to a patient who is not disorganized or psychotic, I understand that the patient has elicited in me a reasonable course of action that, for whatever reason, they have either rejected or not allowed themselves to consider. The stronger my desire to give advice, the more intense the patient's fears of creating this solution on their own. Unless the consequences of the patient's risky and self-injurious actions would be severe, resisting the urge to offer a suggestion is the better choice. Giving unnecessary advice reinforces the patient's devalued sense of self, interferes with growth of their ability to discover, strengthen, and use their own good judgment, and aggrandizes the therapist. Giving unneeded advice may also make it more difficult to explore the unconscious thoughts and emotions that interfered with their arriving at their own solution. Whenever a piece of advice that I have given is accepted, especially when the patient thinks it's a "great idea," I always explore what interfered with their creating that solution.

When a patient, wrestling with a very difficult decision, asks for my advice, a different dilemma is created. If the issue is one in which I do not have expertise, I am strongly inclined not to give advice. In such situations, if I find myself holding a strong opinion about what the best course of action for the patient is, I believe that I am holding an opinion that the patient thinks is best but is stymied about pursuing that course of action by some conflict. Or, they may not even have considered what I am considering.

Regardless of what I choose to say, my position is very likely to be subtly conveyed, either through my tone of voice, cadence, choice of words, facial expression, or other means. Patients become very adept at reading us; nearly every therapist has heard "I can tell that you think I should…" even though they haven't said so explicitly. Whether a patient has read me correctly or incorrectly, I am always curious about what perceptions contributed to their understanding.

◇◇

NO ACTION BY A THERAPIST IS NEUTRAL.

The psychoanalytic literature on the topic of neutrality is diverse and extensive. Recently, Gabbard (2022), Hart (2022), Holmes (2022), and Portuges (2022), explored the topic from the perspective on race and culture, a perspective that was, not long ago, considered outside the purview of psychoanalysis. One aspect of psychoanalysis cannot be neutral. Everything we do, every clinical interaction, either increases the patient's sense of safety, deepens their experience of being understood, and furthers the therapy, or has the opposite impact, reinforcing their need to remain armored and amplifying doubts that they can ever be understood or helped. During much of every psychotherapy session, the impact of our behavior—including quiet, attentive listening—is so subtle and unremarkable that it appears negligible, taken for granted by the therapist and unnoticed by the patient.

These moments, seemingly insignificant, imperceptibly contribute to an atmosphere in which patients feel more confidence in the safety of the relationship, gain greater freedom to say what is on their mind, and facilitate the discovery of what they have hidden from themselves. They further the patient's conviction that they will not be judged, shamed, humiliated, or hurt in other ways by the therapist. Within these unremarkable moments we develop deeper understanding of both the patient and what they elicit in us. These interactions constitute the core of the therapeutic alliance.

Hurtful actions are inevitable in every relationship. Even an ideal psychotherapeutic relationship will give rise to its share of pain. When we make mistakes, including interventions that wound deeply or are so threatening that the patient cannot reflect on them, we know that we have damaged the patient and shaken their trust in us. Just as most of the positive moments that form the bulk of each psychotherapeutic session go unnoticed by analyst and patient, there are also imperceptible moments that are hurtful but never brought into focus.

Others are blunt and direct. One morning I "forgot" to unlock the front door of my office. My first patient knocked loudly and persistently until I heard him. I knew I resented his scorn and was angered by his antisemitic provocations, but I had no idea how burning and consuming my fury and resentment were. The patient immediately understood the meaning of my leaving the door locked. Most hurtful moments are less dramatic. A patient's perception that their therapist has reacted defensively to something they said is a common example.

A balance between these opposing transference and counter-transference reactions always exists. No matter the degree to which the therapist has earned the patient's trust, the patient is continually re-examining whether that trust is genuinely warranted. Although this constant reevaluation is not conscious, it is always present and desirable. If being honest with themselves, all therapists know that they are uncomfortable in some clinical interactions and therefore should expect and respect the patient's subtle caution about being too scornful, too sad, too seductive, too angry....

If the therapist manages a hurtful interaction by acknowledging what has transpired, explores the patient's reactions, and formulates their understanding of what contributed to the experience, the therapeutic relationship will be strengthened. Ironically, if owned and honestly explored by patient and therapist, hurtful experiences provide meaningful ballast that allows the psychotherapeutic ship to better weather the next storm. A therapeutic relationship that appears devoid of such interactions is highly suspect. Both patient and therapist have avoided interactions that would prove the therapist's vulnerability and hurtfulness, or both have been in denial about its presence. Trust that has never been shaken is brittle.

◇◇◇◇◇◇◇◇◇◇◇◇◇◇◇◇◇◇◇◇◇◇◇◇◇◇◇◇◇◇◇◇◇◇◇◇◇◇

THERE IS MORE TO PSYCHOTHERAPY THAN TALKING AND LISTENING.

"Talking about" something with a patient and "listening" to a patient constitute the very essence of psychoanalytic therapy, and yet they are incomplete descriptions of the psychotherapeutic process. The incompleteness reflects an implicit understatement of the degree to which the lives of patient and therapist are interwoven, whether they meet weekly for several months or five times a week for many years. We do not simply talk with and listen to our patients; we live with them each time we meet.

When a patient and I are "talking about" their aggression, whether directed toward me or toward someone else, we are having an "angry conversation." I am not simply talking with them about their anger nor listening to an angry person. In the moment, our relationship has been "aggressivized." Similarly, if the patient is speaking to me about sex, whether it consciously has anything to do with me, our lived experience, our relationship, has been sexualized.

So too with sadness, jealously, fear, or any other affectively charged state of mind the patient brings to a given session. When the patient has drained their talk of any interest and affect, they have asked the therapist to live a bored existence with them. The therapy has become "just talk"; there does not even appear to be anything worthy of listening to. The boring patient is afraid of allowing the therapist to find them interesting and afraid to have interest in discovering the hidden issues with which they struggle.

Were psychotherapy just talking with or just listening to patients, we would be engaged in a very different kind of "being with" the patient, one with considerably less potential for learning, change, growth, and transformation. The very fact that talking with patients means living with them intensively, anxiously, expectantly, uncertainly, sadly, etc., is what makes psychotherapy "work" in both senses of the word. Psychotherapy requires sustained, strong effort from both patient and therapist. If the fit is right, if therapists can understand themselves, the patient, and the process between them well enough and respond helpfully enough, psychotherapy works. The psychotherapeutic relationship, sometimes sexualized, sometimes infused with sorrow, jealousy, and anger, requires strenuous effort from both patient and therapist. That is the work each must expend to ensure that the psychotherapeutic endeavor is as effective as possible.

EVERY THERAPY IS FILLED WITH UNDERSTANDINGS, MISUNDERSTANDINGS, AND MISSED UNDERSTANDINGS.

The practice of psychotherapy depends on the therapist's ever-increasing understanding of the patient and the patient's ever-increasing self-awareness and experience of being "unambivalently understood," a concept I learned from Harold Searles. But every psychotherapy, like every other relationship, has its fair share of misunderstandings which, if they can be explored and corrected, contain the potential to strengthen the relationship and further the progress of the therapy.

A young woman in her late twenties had been in therapy with me for several months. She had experienced other psychotherapies and, before we had begun working together, had started taking an anti-depressant. Her experience with me was quite different in that she found herself giving voice to many intense emotions, which brought her great relief, as well as considerable surprise and some concern.

In early May, I informed her that I would not be meeting with her for the month of August, and, in the sessions that followed, she made no reference to my upcoming absence. In mid-July, she said, "Since you will be gone for a week in August, I will need to get my prescription filled before you go." Surprised when I said that I would be away for the entire month, she said that she had just misunderstood how long I would be on vacation. This misunderstanding was readily corrected and, as we explored it, she realized that she was much more powerfully impacted by my vacation than she realized or wished to be. Although uncertain, she thought my suggestion that the impact of my long absence contributed to her misunderstanding was correct. She emphatically added, "I never want to be dependent on anyone."

A woman in her 40s was well into the fourth year of an analysis which she began because of a significant depression. Her analyst, an extremely fastidious man with an elegantly decorated office, had recently had his couch reupholstered in a beautiful open-weave fabric. At the end of the last hour of the week, the patient, as she sat up on the couch, caught her ring on the fabric and loosened one of the threads. Always vulnerable to feeling criticized and frightened of her analyst's disapproval and anger, she apologized, expressing her deep regret. Still immersed in conveying her concerns, she was startled when the analyst said, "Go!" Feeling chastised and hurt, she left the office and spent the entire weekend consumed with dread of facing him on Monday. The "go" confirmed his disgust and anger with her, and she was tormented by its relentless echoes.

The patient began the Monday session apologizing again, tearfully conveying how frightened she had been by what she experienced as his stern dismissal, "Go." Completely surprised, he insisted that "go" was intended to be reassuring so that she would not torment herself over the weekend. He added that the pulled thread was virtually unnoticeable and insisted that he was not angry with her. The patient was greatly relieved, and the misunderstanding allowed meaningful work regarding her pervasive fear of disapproval and criticism.

One must question whether the analyst's tone of voice might

have resonated with anger, even if he was certain that it did not and sincerely wished to alleviate the patient's distress. Setting that possibility aside and taking him at his word, this is an example of a misunderstanding that caused considerable distress but was able to be clarified and to be used to further the therapy.

A "missed understanding" is a very different interaction. A second-year psychiatric resident had recently begun work with their first outpatient, a 30-year-old man who routinely was 5–10 minutes late for his appointment, always with an explanation which absolved him completely of any responsibility for his lateness. The new baby needed to have his diaper changed while his wife had to get the older child off to school; his car would not start; the traffic was terrible, etc. Not understanding that his lateness was noteworthy and conveyed something important, the therapist, while aware of the pattern, did not identify the lateness as meaningful and needing exploration. Through supervision, they came to understand that the lateness was significant and tactfully drew attention to the patient's consistent tardiness.

Far from feeling criticized, which the resident had feared, the patient said he was aware that he was always late but did not think it warranted mention or had any significance. When the resident suggested that its meaning might be well hidden but significant, the patient began to reflect on that possibility. What emerged was the patient's wish not to feel controlled, not by his parents, his wife, his baby, and not even by the need to get to the airport early. In fact, he got a quiet sense of satisfaction by being just on time to catch a plane and by making his therapist wait, uncertain of when or whether he was going to show up.

This totally unremarkable experience represents what I think of as a "missed understanding," an interaction between therapist and patient which neither understands to have significance and unconscious meaning, or to which both attribute a superficial explanation, while failing to consider the possibility of a hidden, more unsettling meaning. A clinician with greater experience would certainly have understood the importance of the patient's lateness and explored it. In the case with the resident that I described above, as we discussed the patient's concerns, it became clear that, in addition to not understanding that the patient's lateness had meaning, the resident had not been aware that they were quite unsettled by the patient's consistent tardiness which they considered rude and disrespectful.

The understanding developed by patient and therapist was an important beginning to what developed into a very productive psychotherapy. Had the patient's lateness never been explored, this would have been a missed understanding, and the intense preoccupation with control, dominance, and submission, might well have remained unidentified. The impact of the therapy would have been limited, and the therapist would not have understood the significance of their own conflicts regarding power.

A woman in her mid 70s was in the final weeks of a very productive psychotherapy that was ending because the therapist, a very experienced woman, had developed a serious but not life-threatening illness and had decided to retire. Since she knew the therapist was in her late 70s, the patient had anticipated that her retirement was somewhere on the horizon, and it was evident that the therapist was as unhappy with ending the therapy as she was. As the therapy drew to a close, she returned home after her next to last session, frustrated and annoyed with herself for "intellectualizing" during the entire hour and angry with her therapist, whom she cared about deeply, for letting her "get away with it."

This was a missed understanding, one reflecting the patient's wish to sidestep the intense reactions she had to the forced ending of her treatment and the therapist's wish to avoid the patient's thoughts and feelings as well as her own. Neither was conscious of what had transpired in the moment, but the patient, realizing the significance of her unemotional discussion, brought it to the therapist's attention in the following and final session, and the matter was meaningfully explored.

Missed understandings are remarkably common—often never recognized by patient or therapist—and have powerful ramifications. To the patient, the therapist's "missing," being unaware of the camouflaged meaning of the experience, often indicates that they do not *want* to understand what is transpiring between them. This conclusion is not conscious, but the patient "knows" what they have communicated and "knows" that the therapist, because of their own conflicts and blind spots, has not understood its significance despite listening closely. A missed understanding is an unrecognized, unconscious countertransference reaction, an instance in which the strength of the therapist's personal self blocked an understanding of the patient's concern. Many missed understandings are never recognized but, thankfully, patients are remarkably persistent in bringing important, if skillfully hidden material for us to understand, interpret, and help them to adapt to in a more productive way.

We may miss the opportunity to understand the first time around, and maybe the second and third as well. But we will likely get repeated opportunities, and if the meaning can be clarified, interpreted, and integrated into the patient's sense of self and the therapeutic relationship, there is both relief and the potential for growth. When the communication is not understood, it becomes woven into the fabric of the analysis, unconsciously reinforcing the patient's fear that they are "too much" for the therapist.

When a missed understanding is recognized and explored, the patient's self-understanding deepens but, ironically, they have to absorb the knowledge that they have experienced one of the therapist's vulnerabilities. That may make the therapist "more human," but the awareness and experience of the therapist's vulnerability is always unsettling for the patient and, in a different way, for the therapist as well. Missed understandings can be thought of as "off-stage enactments" (Chused 2003; Busch 2006), and are inevitable in any meaningful psychotherapy. Off-stage enactments can be contrasted with "on-stage enactments" such as described above in which I "forgot" to unlock my door, shutting the patient out. If not recognized and explored, the patient unconsciously but correctly concludes that the therapist wishes to remain unaware of their own avoidance. Patients are always assessing what aspects of themselves are genuinely welcomed into the therapeutic relationship. Each instance in which the therapist refutes the patient's concern that their communication's importance will be unrecognized, ignored, and avoided, reinforces the security of the relationship and reduces the patient's fear of self-awareness.

THE "GOOD'" PSYCHOTHERAPEUTIC SESSION IS A SEDUCTIVE CONCEPT.

"Good" psychotherapeutic sessions are slyly seductive. When the patient's and the therapist's work together results in an unconscious thought or affect being brought to light or a vexing problem burdening the patient being solved, both have a sense of accomplishment and gratitude. After such a session, both will experience deep satisfaction and a desire that subsequent sessions be equally "productive." Such clinical moments are experienced by both parties to be "good," implicitly implying that other therapy hours are less productive, undesirable, and indicative of shortcoming by patient, therapist, or both.

But psychotherapeutic relationships, like all enduring relationships, will be enjoyable, stimulating, boring, eye-opening, surprising, unpleasant, hostile, sexually exciting, tense, confusing, tender, disappointing.... If successful, the psychotherapeutic process that is rooted in the unique conversations we call psychotherapy will involve contentious sessions, "wasted" sessions, sessions that are exasperating in their confusion or boredom, sexually arousing sessions, and sessions that are just plain nasty. Therapists may be tempted to work hard to ensure that sessions do not end with the patient feeling disappointed (Schafer 1999), frustrated, angry, or in tears. Patients may criticize the therapist for "not working hard enough" or not being skilled enough to alleviate their distress. Therapists and patients may sometimes unconsciously avoid addressing the patient's criticism and feelings of dissatisfaction. And then, often finding themselves at loggerheads, fear they are at an impasse.

When the sources of the patient's pain are uncertain, when the solution to some problem is unclear, the therapist cannot simply exert greater effort to facilitate the progress of the therapy. Tolerating the frustration both are experiencing, patiently listening for and trying to identify obstacles to acquiring greater understanding, is extremely difficult work. Often, the therapist is not clear what specific conflicts are generating the patient's distress and must accept the patient's frustration. Even if the therapist believes that they do understand the issues at play, they must accept and respect their inability to alleviate the patient's suffering, disappointment, and frustration. "Today was a total waste of time and money," may ring in the therapist's ear long after the patient sourly closes or slams the door.

I have often become painfully aware of a strong desire to do something to transform a "bad" hour into a "good" one, especially when the patient and I have experienced a string of them. This has always reflected an omnipotent wish that I could somehow protect both myself and the patient from these very unsettling sessions that seem not only unproductive but harmful. It is hard to resist wracking one's brain in hopes of figuring something out or taking a shot at an intervention wishing that the patient will feel some relief and one's disappointment with oneself will ease. Consciously or unconsciously, patients often blame the therapist, themselves, or both for wasted, frustrating sessions.

Many patients find it difficult to tolerate the tension and apprehension of experiencing this bitter disappointment and fear, sometimes unconscious, that the therapist cannot help them. They may also be very concerned that, in fact, no therapist can address their difficulties. The therapist may struggle to live with feeling inadequate, holding themselves responsible for the patient's unhappiness.

Over the course of an extended, successful psychotherapy, both patient and therapist learn to endure any number of "unproductive" psychotherapeutic hours and to respect that they are unavoidable, meaningful aspects of the therapy which, if lived with and explored, will facilitate growth. When such a state of affairs persists for a long period of time, the impasse is best resolved by the therapist's own supervision or by the patient having a consultation with another psychotherapist.

David I Joseph MD

✧✧✧✧✧✧✧✧✧✧✧✧✧✧✧✧✧✧✧✧✧✧✧✧✧✧✧✧✧✧✧✧✧✧✧✧✧

TRANSFERENCE AND COUNTERTRANSFERENCE ARE NOT NOUNS.

Since Freud's discovery (1905) that a patient's unconscious experience of the therapist can powerfully shape and even destroy the treatment, understanding and resolving the "transference" has been central to psychoanalytic psychotherapy. What is usually referred to as "the transference" is a condensed reference to what Freud understood to be the patient's transference *reactions* to him. These reactions allowed him to experience and better understand aspects of the patient's childhood experiences and adaptive mechanisms that were unconsciously being given expression within the psychoanalytic relationship. Transference reactions and their counterpart, the therapist's countertransference reactions, became an important focus in Freud's subsequent work and have become even more central in psychoanalytic practice today.

"Transference" is a poster child for demonstrating the ways in which etymology can enrich our understanding of the current meanings of words, meanings that are hidden in the history of the word, itself. "Transference" derives from two Latin words, *trans*, meaning "over," and *ferro*, meaning "to make." Linguistically, a transference reaction is a makeover of some earlier relationship. In the conjugation of *ferro*, the past participle is *latum*. Therefore, transference is linguistically and psychologically a translation, a translation of the private experience of an extremely important relationship, including traumatic relationships, that shapes and is being lived in a current relationship. The Greek word for transference is *metaphor*, and a transference reaction can also be usefully conceptualized as a metaphor for another relationship. Transference reactions are not repetitions; they are new creations (Loewald 1960; Poland 1992) that translate and metaphorically allow greater understanding of unconscious reactions to emotionally charged experiences and significant relationships.

Transference reactions are the creative soul of the patient's story as they experience it in psychotherapy. Transference reactions are most certainly not the only way in which patients express and facilitate understanding of their unconscious thoughts, emotions, and experiences. Dreams, slips of the tongue, "acting out," and other unconsciously motivated actions do so as well. But transference reactions, when understood to be translations and metaphors, provide a rich opportunity for patients to discover and understand how their reactions to past experiences are vibrantly alive and shape their present experience of themselves and others.

Every patient's story is shaped by and filled with unconscious thoughts and emotions, but patient and therapist are co-writing their own story, their own drama, that expresses the psychotherapeutic life they are creating and live together. This story is truly co-created (Beebe and Lachman 2002). Patient and therapist contribute to the storyline and the demarcation of each separate "chapter." Therapists, too, have transference reactions to the patient. I will explore these reactions later in the discussion of enactments and psychotherapeutic mistakes, but these reactions, many of which never become the object of exploration either within the therapy sessions or in the privacy of the therapist's mind, powerfully shape all aspects of the experience we call psychotherapy.

History is, linguistically and psychologically, a story, "his story," and I have only recently come to appreciate the profound linguistic implications of the word. Historical research, scientific research, and the research that we call psychotherapy facilitate the discovery of new information that is incorporated into a new story, a deeper, enriched history (Schafer 1992). A good writer, be they novelist, poet, historian or physicist, is a good storyteller. Together, a "good enough" analyst working collaboratively with a "good enough" patient author a powerful, memorable story, the story of an entirely unique psychoanalysis.

Transference reactions can be considered from multiple perspectives. To what degree do they reflect prior experiences that have conditioned the person to expect specific responses from their therapist? To what degree are they the product of the patient's inborn sense of vulnerability that they have wrestled with all their life? How important are the patient's projections in shaping their experience of the therapist? To what degree do they arise from the developing relationship with the therapist and reflect something about the therapist which the patient has accurately perceived?

Every relationship is influenced by prior relationships with parents, siblings, mentors, and others who have had a meaningful impact on our lives. What we have absorbed, what we have learned, what we have integrated from these prior relationships shapes and is unconsciously woven into the developing relationship with the therapist. This process of "transferring" influences all our relationships, but, while transferring is an integral aspect of all relationships, transference reactions are not. Transference reactions, as I understand them, are characterized by an intensity of affect and a relatively fixed experience of the other that do not appear to be warranted.

While writing this book, I was immersed in Walter Isaacson's biography of Steve Jobs and was struck by how often Isaacson noted that Jobs, who had a very powerful reaction to learning that he was adopted, was continuously searching for a father figure. No bright line distinguishes a transference reaction from a reaction less strongly influenced by past experience, but movie stars, Nobel prize winners, teachers, and therapists know, sometimes only in a visceral way, that they are the object of a transference reaction.

Over the years, "transference reaction" has become condensed and is now most often referred to as "the transference." Psychotherapists may be inclined to discount the possibility that the patient is reacting strongly to some specific aspect of them. For a psychotic person that "something" can be quite impersonal. When I was a psychiatric resident, one of my patients believed that when I wore a blue necktie I was commenting on her masculinity and when I wore a red necktie I was affirming her femininity. Others may be deeply impacted by a generic aspect of the therapist: age, gender, race, accent, manner of dress, or any other "objective" aspect of their person, but the meaning of this characteristic is created entirely by the patient.

As Merton Gill (1979) stressed, it is extremely important to inquire of the patient whether they experienced anything about us that elicited a response that we understand to be a "transference" reaction. Such an inquiry often elicits the answer, "nothing," sometimes a very surprising response. Regardless of the patient's answer, asking the question encourages therapists to undertake a more rigorous examination of themselves, searching to determine whether something about them contributed to the patient's transference reaction. Asking the question also implicitly indicates to the patient that their experience of the therapist is not necessarily "all in their head." Even if neither patient nor therapist is able to determine what has elicited the transference reaction, understanding that the patient's feelings and thoughts may be responses to some aspect of the therapist is beneficial for both. Asking the question also implicitly underscores the therapist's understanding of the centrality of the interpersonal dimension in all psychotherapy.

At any given moment in a psychotherapy, there are multiple transference reactions that are central to the therapeutic relationship. One transference reaction, however, is usually dominant at a particular time; others will become more apparent in different sessions or future stages of the therapy. Psychoanalytic psychotherapy, especially when the patient has frequent sessions and the dialogue with the therapist is fluid and unedited, facilitates the experience by both patient and therapist of these less conscious but powerfully influential transference reactions and allows them to be better understood from the perspective of earlier relationships.

The aliveness of these reactions creates an opportunity to explore the origins and impact of the unconscious thoughts and emotions that have contributed to the patient's suffering. If the therapeutic relationship is structured properly, there is no need to do anything to encourage or deepen the development of transference reactions. The basic structure of the therapy nurtures their expression.

A psychotherapist may periodically be inclined to encourage the patient to think more about the relationship between them, but this frame of mind reflects his own countertransference reaction to the patient's avoidance or disavowal of the centrality of the therapeutic relationship. The therapist who feels a need to draw attention to "the transference" is responding to the patient's wish to avoid being aware of and thinking about the relationship with their analyst at all, much less have it become central to the work. The patient's reluctance, often surprisingly entrenched, *is* the most prominent transference reaction at the moment. The patient is proclaiming insistently, that their relationship with the therapist is not of much, if any, significance. When this dynamic is active, the therapist's initial focus should be on understanding the patient's avoidance and denial.

Condensing "transference reaction" to "transference" has contributed to a mindset in which interpreting the transference is revered and becomes the primary, if not the sole focus for the interventions by the analyst. I have thought that some psychoanalysts approach *the transference* as a kind of fetish. Implicit in their thinking is the conviction that exploring and interpreting other conflicts and emotionally painful situations in the patient's life will not facilitate meaningful understanding or enduring change and may be used to avoid exploring the therapeutic relationship.

That said, I do believe that understanding and change are most powerfully facilitated when the issues are alive in the moment and in the relationship between patient and therapist. A patient with a phobia of elevators can reduce their dread by reading tomes about elevators and exploring their fears with the therapist. These discussions may allow them to develop the courage to step into an elevator without riding it, or perhaps riding in an elevator with the therapist. Those efforts will not come close to emulating the terror that is certain to occur when they take their first ride alone and watch with terror as the doors slowly shut, possibly trapping them forever. Desensitization in psychoanalysis shares much with the process of desensitization in the cognitive behavioral therapies (Wachtel 1977), an overlap that may be unrecognized by the analyst, as though it would devalue psychoanalysis. When the relationship with the analyst is so intense and filled with conflict that it dominates the moment, the potential for change, for more effective desensitization, is greatest.

When the therapist is not dismissive, critical, intrusive, frightened, excited, or shaming, when some dreaded transference reaction has not materialized, meaningful change is facilitated. Exploring the patient's reactions to sharing their secrets allows their unspoken and frequently unrecognized transference reactions to be modified by the affirming response of the quietly listening, empathic, consistently present therapist. Overemphasis on the patient's relationship with the therapist can lead the patient to believe that the therapist does not appreciate or sufficiently value the importance of other relationships in the patient's life.

A patient's transference reactions and a therapist's counter-transference reactions are commonly designated either "positive" or "negative." Both terms seem to me to be strikingly impersonal, evoking the polarities of electrical current rather than the complex, nuanced subtleties of human experience. I find the categories of "nurturing" and "destructive" to be far more evocative of the experience they describe. Nurturing reactions include validating, affirming, respecting, supporting, understanding, accepting, liking, loving, celebrating, encouraging, praising, congratulating, etc. Destructive reactions include withholding, competing, undermining, criticizing, disrespecting, rejecting, disliking, attacking, hating, discouraging, shaming, humiliating, punishing, mocking, scorning, seducing, etc. As noted earlier, nothing is neutral in psychotherapy; to some degree, every action of the therapist either furthers or inhibits the progress of the therapy. Similarly, transference and countertransference reactions are never neutral; they are always either nurturing or hurtful and destructive.

Patients locked in a consistently "negative" transference reaction are armoring themselves against some feared assault or bitter disappointment and are willing to forgo the care they yearn for which would grow from a less defended stance. They may also be protecting against the dangers of loving and being loved. These individuals may experience a respectful, nurturing relationship to be so infused with vulnerability and danger as to be almost unimaginable. Such threats are deeply rooted in unconscious fantasy, very resistant to change, and rationalized in ways that are compelling to the patient. Patients with a resolutely nurturing transference reaction are protecting themselves and the therapist from threats posed by their scornful, nasty, suspicious, traits. Transference reactions also involve projective mechanisms in which patients focus on unconscious aspects of themselves that they experience as existing in the therapist. For patients dominated by an intense destructive transference reaction, their concern about destroying a loved and loving object can be difficult to bring into focus. This dynamic is captured in the joke about the child who killed their parents and asked the judge for mercy because they were an orphan.

∞∞∞∞∞∞∞∞∞∞∞∞∞∞∞∞∞∞∞∞∞∞∞∞∞∞∞∞∞∞∞∞∞

BEING A PSYCHOTHERAPIST IS LONELY: PSYCHOANALYTIC LISTENING, PSYCHOANALYTIC ALONENESS, AND PSYCHOANALYTIC LONELINESS.

I have seen
A curious child, who dwelt upon a tract
Of inland ground, applying to his ear
The convolutions of a smooth-lipped shell,
To which, in silence hushed, his very soul
Listened intensely; and his countenance soon
Brightened with joy, for from within were heard
Murmurings, whereby the monitor expressed
Mysterious union with its native sea.
William Wordsworth, *The Excursion*, 191–192

At its core, every relationship is a cross-cultural experience. Psychoanalysis is a unique, intimate, ever-evolving relationship between two individuals, each with their own conscious and unconscious mind and culture, rooted in and nourished by the genetic-biological-familial-sociocultural environment in which they developed. To be productive, the culture of the patient-therapist relationship requires an enduring experience of safety and respect. Within such a relationship, the patient can overcome the vulnerability inherent in associating freely, allowing the therapist to understand them and to use that understanding to alleviate their distress and facilitate change.

Every psychotherapy is a voyage of discovery for both patient and therapist. Wordsworth lyrically and evocatively conveys the universal desire and unspoken impossibility of fully knowing another and, by implication, the desire and impossibility of being fully understood by another or completely understanding one-self. The analyst, like Wordsworth's child, listens with their soul (psyche) and tries to resonate with the soul of their patient, with its prose and its passion. The "mysterious union" of the shell with its "native sea," evokes the unquenchable human thirst for immersion in the sea of the maternal object, a desire that powerfully shapes the psychotherapeutic relationship for both patient and therapist.

In his preface to the *Lyrical Ballads*, Wordsworth said:

> In spite of the difference of soil and climate, of language and manners, of laws and customs, in spite of things silently gone out of mind and violently destroyed, the Poet binds together by passion and knowledge, the vast empire of human society as it is spread over the whole earth, and over all time. The objects of the Poet's thoughts are everywhere; though the eyes and senses of man are, it is true, his favorite guides, yet he will follow wheresoever he can find an atmosphere of sensation in which to move his wings.

A psychoanalyst, listening to Wordsworth, might be moved to discover sensations that allow movement of their wings, to create and convey their deepest understanding. While, for the therapist, this state of mind is especially apparent when listening to dreams, the patient's and their own, it shapes everything that passes between them. "Freely" associating and psychoanalytic listening are subtly but meaningfully altered states of consciousness, imbued with fluidity, understanding, and creativity.

However well-attuned we may become—musicality and harmony being a useful metaphor—and no matter how deeply patients feel we know them, their desire to be totally understood inevitably encounters the intense disappointment inherent in existential separateness. The therapists, too, must accept the disappointment that the depth of knowing their patient, their relationship, and themselves is limited.

Achieving mutual understanding is only possible through the negotiation of meaning. To negotiate meaning with someone, you have to become aware of and respect the differences in your backgrounds and when these differences are important. You need enough diversity of cultural and personal experience to be aware that divergent world views exist and what they might be like. You also need patience, a certain flexibility in world view, and a general tolerance for mistakes, as well as a talent for finding the right metaphor to communicate the relevant parts of unshared experiences or to highlight the shared experiences while deemphasizing the others.

Metaphorical imagination is a crucial skill in creating rapport and in communicating the nature of unshared experience. This skill exists, in large measure, of the ability to bend your world view and adjust the way you categorize your world experience. Problems of mutual understanding are not exotic; they arise in all extended conversations where meaning is important.

When it really counts, meaning is almost never communicated via the conduit of metaphor, that is, where one person transmits a fixed, clear proposition to another by means of expression in a common language, where both parties have all the relevant common knowledge, assumptions, values, etc. When the chips are down, meaning is negotiated...." (Lakoff and Johnson 1999, 231)

Shared understanding and shared meaning are created by patient and therapist in the generative space in which they are negotiated. Much of the negotiating process occurs unconsciously, but the process of negotiating meaning is neither exotic nor mystical. Negotiating psychoanalytic meaning requires mutual commitment, respect, uncertainty, doubt, trust, imagination, playfulness, humor, self-reflection, and courage.

Being a therapist powerfully stimulates the desire to have someone attuned to and listening to them the way they listen to their patients, a state of mind I think of as psychoanalytic loneliness. Psychoanalytic loneliness is distinct and separate from analytic aloneness. Analytic aloneness is rooted in the need to keep our therapeutic lives completely private and confidential, and to keep our private lives separate from our patients.

Ironically, the profound intimacy that develops between analyst and patient does not temper the pain of psychoanalytic loneliness. It seems quite possible to me that the longing to alleviate this loneliness contributes to boundary violations, both sexual and non-sexual.

Aloneness, itself, is a neutral experience, but the meaning with which we imbue it engenders a range of emotions. Aloneness can be sought, enjoyed, used for learning, and transformed into a private, contemplative, creative space. Aloneness can also be infused with unbearably painful emotions and thoughts of rejection, repulsiveness, and unlovability. Or it can be saturated with fears that one's sadness, anger, scorn, jealousy, and desire to be loved are too much for anyone to tolerate or endure, much less welcome.

Ironically, accepting that one can never be fully known nor fully know oneself is desirable and reassuring. Such awareness attests to our existence as separate individuals, responsible for and "free" to conduct our lives as we wish, possessing private thoughts, feelings, and fantasies, not controlled by others or by our wish to immerse ourselves in another. I have placed "free" in quotations because each of us lives with the illusion that we are less influenced by our unconscious mind than we truly are. Embracing and valuing the "oneness" and "twoness" of human existence (Poland 2018) is one of the most meaningful accomplishments of a productive psychotherapy.

◇◇◇◇◇◇◇◇◇◇◇◇◇◇◇◇◇◇◇◇◇◇◇◇◇◇◇◇◇◇◇◇◇◇◇◇◇

TAKING NOTES DOESN'T ALWAYS INTERFERE WITH PSYCHOANALYTIC LISTENING AND PSYCHOANALYTIC REMEMBERING.

Earlier in this book, I mentioned that I never take notes when meeting with a patient (except during initial sessions, when I am likely to learn a great deal of historical and medical information). Trying to be an accurate recorder interferes with my ability to listen psychoanalytically. My hearing remains acute, but my listening is significantly impaired. I cannot maintain the fluid attention required to understand the patient's immediate concerns, begin to get a sense of underlying issues, and respond in the most empathic way to their words, tone of voice, physical expressiveness, and language. I also cannot create the space that nurtures my own freely associating, personal state of reverie—my private, often wordless responses—which so powerfully shape the essence of the psychoanalytic dialogue.

Some psychoanalytic therapists whom I respect knit or do needlework during sessions. As a former pipe smoker (fiddler), I know that such activity can facilitate a state of psychoanalytic listening, but these activities require a very different quality of psychological attention than note taking. And, of course, whether they say anything or not, patients are acutely aware of when we are taking notes and when our writing stops, drawing conclusions about what we have found important enough to record.

When I was a psychoanalytic candidate in the 1970s, I did

not know anyone who took notes during sessions. Notes written afterwards were deemed more than sufficient, although I had one supervisor who preferred that I take no notes at all, even after the session. By the late 1990s, I was surprised to realize that nearly all psychoanalytic candidates who met with me for supervision came with detailed notes taken during each clinical hour. What accounted for this change remains a mystery. Whenever a therapist in supervision prefers to take verbatim notes during the therapeutic session, I explain that, in my opinion, whatever may be gained by having a more "accurate" recounting of what transpired in the session is significantly outweighed by what is lost by the limitations imposed on listening.

I always thought I made a really good case for taking notes after each session, but several supervisees continued their note taking. Over time I came to realize that, without thorough notes taken during the session, they feared they would not remember the clinical material in enough detail and therefore would convey an inaccurate sense of the session, and that the absence of notes would make it difficult to maintain the continuity of the analysis. Some seemed concerned that I would pass harsh judgment on their faulty memory.

After supervising psychoanalytic candidates for several years, I realized that, for some, taking notes created a calmer state of mind and facilitated better psychoanalytic listening. Without the burden of remembering, they found it easier to maintain a fluid state of mind, the opposite impact that taking notes has on me. For a few, the altered state of consciousness characteristic of evenly hovering attention elicited a degree of anxiety that interfered with their ability to listen psychoanalytically. For these individuals, taking notes served an organizing function. My assumption that taking notes could only interfere with treatment was just plain wrong.

The process of remembering within the psychoanalytic dialogue is wondrous and endlessly fascinating. Psychoanalytic remembering is created in the minds of patient and therapist by the immediate experience of each within the psychotherapeutic conversation. Listening psychoanalytically requires that one attempt to keep one's mind fully open to remembering without "trying" to remember. I sometimes take notes after a session that appears especially meaningful or that I think I may want to draw upon for teaching or writing, but I never review any notes prior to a given hour, even if the patient and I have agreed that something which occurred at the end of the previous session warrants further exploration.

Other than using the ten-minute break between patients to "clear my mind," I do not prepare for a psychoanalytic session the way I do for a class. Beginning each session fresh, with shared experience but at the same time "without memory or desire" (Bion 1967) and always open to being surprised, is, for me, another aspect of creating an organic psychoanalytic relationship.

David I Joseph MD

THE PSYCHOANALYTIC FRAME PROTECTS THE INTERNAL PSYCHOANALYTIC FRAMEWORK.

Early in the process of writing this book, I was completely caught off guard when I realized that something troubled me about the concept of the psychoanalytic frame. Until that point, I was quite content with Robert Langs' (1978) metaphor of a frame for psychoanalytic therapy. It is precise, necessary, useful, and readily understood. It provides an essential boundary that contains the relationship between patient and analyst, protecting the analysis from harmfully evolving into some other kind of relationship. Among its essential components are privacy and confidentiality, a schedule of sessions, and determination of fee and payment. When clearly defined and rigorously maintained, the frame guards against a range of crossings, often subtle, that can damage patient, analyst, and therapy. The elements of the psychoanalytic frame suggest the meticulous procedures for insuring a sterile "operating room." In both situations, the procedures are essential to protect the patient and ensure an uncontaminated operating room.

These aspects of the psychoanalytic frame also suggest the dimensions and physical components of a picture frame. Selecting the frame for a painting, however, requires attention to the nature of the picture as well as its dimensions. In selecting a frame, a framer will be sensitive to the subject and aesthetics of the picture as well as by its size. A well-chosen frame provides a boundary for

146

the painting without distracting the viewer and subtly enhances the impact of the artwork.

The initial "picture" of the patient, however, changes soon after patient and therapist meet and constantly evolves as the therapy progresses. A therapist begins each treatment with the same frame, but, as the picture of the patient takes shape, the psychoanalytic "aesthetics" of the analyst's frame change in response to the "picture" of the patient in the mind of the therapist. While it is tempting to be more specific about what the "aesthetics of the psychoanalytic frame" suggest, simply allowing it to be an evocative metaphor seems preferable. In a productive psychotherapy, therapists will develop a different picture of the patient and themselves, and patients will paint a different picture of themselves and the therapist.

Frame has another definition: the "timbers, joists, etc. forming the skeleton of a building" (OED), and these constitute a very different and equally essential element of any psychoanalytic psychotherapy, an aspect that I think of as its framework. Each therapist has their own personal, relatively unchanging psychotherapeutic framework that they bring to every session with every patient. Among the structural elements which every therapist builds into their framework are: consistency, timeliness, an openness to listen to whatever the patient needs to discuss, a non-judgmental frame of mind, and a rigorous commitment to privacy and confidentiality. In the framework the therapist also includes that the patient is suffering and feels vulnerable, the importance of developing and maintaining a space of safety, an enduring respect for patients' need to reveal and discover aspects of themselves at their own pace, and a conviction about the power of psychoanalysis to facilitate meaningful change. The psychoanalytic framework includes understanding the patient's yearning for closeness but also an essential affirmation of the patient's "otherness" (Poland 2000).

Education, experience, and expertise notwithstanding, the therapist's psychotherapeutic framework includes the conviction that therapist and patient are always negotiating meaning within their relationship. Every interpretation, no matter the therapist's years of experience, is understood to be only a hypothesis, a hypothesis offered with a range of convictions. Every therapist has a psychoanalytic framework that includes an unspoken, deep commitment to remain fully present, to allow themselves to know the patient as fully as possible while also allowing themselves to be known by the patient within the context of the psychotherapeutic relationship. The psychoanalytic frame shields patient and therapist from the expectable changes in the weather. The therapist's personal framework must be strong and flexible enough to withstand gale force psychoanalytic winds and sometimes a psychoanalytic earthquake which are common in a meaningful psychoanalysis.

Every patient comes to an initial psychotherapeutic meeting with hopes that their distress can be alleviated. Even if they have never had a psychotherapeutic relationship, they meet the therapist having imagined something about what will transpire and, if they have had some prior experience in psychotherapy, with a template constructed from their prior psychotherapeutic relationships. From the initial meeting, however, therapist and patient begin to fashion a framework for their work together which is integrated with the therapist's personal framework.

The maintenance of the psychotherapeutic frame is solely the responsibility of the therapist. All patients, including experienced psychotherapists, experience powerful desires to transform the relationship into one that offers different gratifications, be it an early maternal experience, an extra-therapeutic friendship, a romantic relationship, a sexual liaison, a violent competition, or an all-out war with a hated enemy. The therapist, and the therapist alone, has the challenging task of maintaining the frame and of using their knowledge, experience, and expertise to resist and analyze the patient's persistent, intense efforts to transform the relationship so that it will meet unfulfilled childhood needs, a transformation that would destroy the therapeutic endeavor for both.

Architects and psychotherapists have much in common. Unless the client allows the architect to know them, to understand what kinds of space they want to live in, architect and client cannot work together productively. Like the relationship between therapist and patient, the relationship between architect and client is both personally meaningful and very professional. A psychotherapist cannot develop a good working relationship and productive psychotherapy with every patient. An architect will not be able to work creatively and productively with every client. Patients hope that we can help them remodel themselves. They feel ill at ease in the psychological space in which they live, often in ways difficult to convey. They have inhabited this space for so long that envisioning an alternative, let alone making substantial changes, feels unimaginable and unsettling. Building a new psychological home is impossible; the existing structure and lot dimensions limit aspects of the remodeling, a disappointing but inherent aspect of the process.

The architect, as they get to know their client better, develops an image of what is desired and what is possible. As the psychotherapist gets to know their patient, they develop an image of who the patient can become. This image becomes a central, usually wordless, aspect of the psychotherapeutic process and relation-ship. A house can be remodeled with no or minimal changes to the exterior, but with significant interior changes. So, too, can patients transform themselves with profound interior changes, but little or no change apparent to others.

While the metaphors of frame and framework are meaningful and useful, the metaphor of a living, miraculously adaptable, semi-permeable membrane, the cell wall, and the biological workings of the interior components of a cell are, for me, much more evocative of the psychoanalytic experience. The adaptable construction of the cell wall facilitates the introduction of everything the cell needs to survive and fulfill its function. The cell wall regulates its channels to allow the entrance of nutrients and the excretion of substances that disturb its equilibrium. Within a cell, structures like the nucleus, mitochondria, and endoplasmic reticulum have distinct metabolic functions and work in concert to promote growth. The threat of toxins is ever present and threaten its very existence. The metaphor of a cell reflects the aliveness and adaptability of psychoanalytic therapy, emphasizing that each party contributes to the creation, modifications, and outcome of the psychoanalytic experience. Both analyst and patient live and grow within the psychoanalytic cell. Psychotherapy is very much an organic experience.

<><><><><><><><><><><><><><><><><><><><><><><><><><><><>

IT IS PARADOXICAL THAT THERAPISTS RESPECT THEIR PATIENTS.

The desire to be respected and admired is powerfully present within each of us, so powerfully that I think of it as a drive. Each patient, deeply immersed in the process of psychotherapy, is ever wrestling with the concern that they will speak or behave in some way that jeopardizes their therapist's respect, whether the actions relate to past experiences, deeply infused with shame and guilt, or current fantasies and desires. And yet, the patient also wants to share these painful shame and guilt-filled experiences and fantasies, knowing that the changes they wish to accomplish will be significantly limited should they keep them private.

Sometimes the shame is entirely warranted; the patient has acted illegally, unethically, violently, or abusively and expects that confessing their behavior will elicit the therapist's silent disapproval, even if the patient has little or no concern that the therapist will express their disapproval explicitly. In fact, if the therapist were actually neutral about an act that undoubtedly warranted disapproval, the patient's trust in and respect for their therapist's values and personal ethics would be seriously tarnished.

Neutrality, so central to psychoanalytic work, does not mean that the therapist acts as though they were ethically neutered. Rather, what the patient requires is continued acceptance by the therapist, an acceptance that does not deny or dilute aspects of themselves that warrant shame and/or guilt. Also required is an enduring commitment to help the patient achieve understanding and transformation of the underlying, unconscious motivations that resulted in the shameful, guilty actions and fantasies. The therapist's judgments, rarely explicit, become woven into the patient-therapist relationship. Sometimes, the patient's shame or guilt is unwarranted, instilled by a parent, religion, or culture whose condemnation of some specific behavior (e.g., masturbation, homosexuality, alcohol use, abortion, emotional display, etc.) has been absorbed by the patient.

The patient, however, has often distorted their experience of their parents and their sociocultural world by projecting their own searing self-condemnation onto them, thus experiencing them and the world as harsher and more unforgiving. In such situations, the patient's transference reactions will generate a sense of pervasive vulnerability that makes exploration of these experiences and discovery of their unconscious motivations fraught with danger. In these moments, healing is rooted in the therapist's acknowledgment of the patient's actions, shame, and guilt, empathic understanding, and continued acceptance of the person who has shouldered the painful, difficult work of being a patient. Central to the effectiveness of the psychotherapy is the therapist's silent understanding that the patient's shame and guilt are, to some degree, warranted.

As I briefly discussed earlier, our respect for the patient is ironically strengthened when they find the courage to share shameful and guilt-infused aspects of themselves with us, sometimes including past actions that are unethical or illegal. At the same time the patient loses our respect with regard to the behavior (tormenting a sibling, defrauding Medicare, assaulting a spouse, sexually abusing a child, etc.), they simultaneously earn our increased respect because they have so successfully fulfilled the job of being a patient. Being a patient, in the context of being in therapy, is their job, and we respect them for "doing a good job, not for being a good person." Respect for the patient is also ironically earned when he mocks, attacks, or tortures us. Jonathan Lear (2004) has written eloquently about the importance of irony in constructing a meaningful and satisfying life. Irony is also very much at the center of constructing a meaningful and satisfying psychotherapy.

A central element of the trust that we earn from patients is the trust that we will not rub salt in psychological wounds that already burn with shame, mortification, and guilt. The patient's trust of the therapist includes the knowledge, unverbalized and usually unconsciously conceptualized, that our respect for them has been deepened and strengthened by virtue of how seriously and successfully he has met the demands of being a patient.

Janet Malcolm (1981) captured the public's attention when she described the impossibilities of one analyst's professional life and popularized the notion that psychoanalysis, itself, is an "impossible profession." The job of being a patient may seem impossible, too. If they share their shame and guilt, if they are ruthlessly honest, how can they possibly earn the deep respect and love they crave? And yet, this seeming impossibility is central to any meaningful psychoanalysis.

The corresponding aspect of respect in the psychotherapeutic relationship involves the patient's respect for the therapist. This respect is nurtured by a range of the therapist's actions, many of which are contained in Schafer's (1983) exploration of the "analytic attitude" and in my earlier discussion of the psychoanalytic frame and framework. How consistently the therapist keeps their psychoanalytic balance under the constant pressure of the patient's transference reactions will contribute to patient's respect for them.

An additional, important, and easily overlooked element of respect which the therapist earns (or loses) is rooted in the way in which they respond to their own inevitable "mistakes" and the ways in which these mistakes are owned (or disavowed) and allowed to be explored within the therapy. There are many categories of mistakes, ranging from billing errors and double booking, to yelling at or having a sexual relationship with a patient. To some extent, any mistake (I include "enactments" as one category of mistake) will elicit feelings of shame and, to the degree that the patient has been hurt by the mistake, guilt. This is true even if the mistake can be understood and explored in a manner that genuinely advances the therapy. Ironically, the immediacy of these moments in which the therapist's blind spots and vulnerability are evident, allows a degree of insight and understanding for both therapist and patient that is transformative.

Jeff and I started analytic training together and became close friends. It didn't take long before we learned that we shared the same analyst, Dr. M. Several years later, still in the midst of classes, our analyst raised my fee. In a biting, challenging tone, I asked Dr. M whether he had also raised Jeff's fee. The immediate answer was "No," he had not because Jeff could not afford it.

My instantaneous, explosive reaction was to accuse him of favoring Jeff and ask that I fund part of Jeff's analysis. Dr. M reflexively (or so it seemed to me) said he had made a mistake in telling me anything about Jeff's fee. My injury was compounded when my insistence that I must have done something to provoke his "mistake" was met with steadfast denial. Could I have believed Dr. M's conviction, I would have been greatly relieved, but my skepticism not only persisted, but was actually increased by his denial.

Only a number of years after the end of my analysis did I find the mental space and courage to hypothesize, with considerable conviction, that Dr. M had difficulty identifying the very subtle but deeply hurtful wounds I had inflicted. Of equal importance, I came to understand that he was also unable to find and claim his own wish to retaliate, a desire powerful enough to generate "the mistake." I was frightened of my unknown, harshly judgmental qualities and hidden nastiness, although I was enough aware of them to be certain I must have provoked him. Only many years later did I come to have some understanding of how I had subtly and very powerfully provoked him, but I believe that Dr. M's blind spot had made it more difficult for me to discover, own, understand, and address my sadism.

Whether accurate or not, I held this conviction, and the consequent erosion of my respect for him remained a sorrowful aspect of my psychoanalysis, an analysis that was deeply meaningful and transformative in many ways. Had Dr. M been able to discover and acknowledge that he had blinded himself to my subtle cruelty and that his wish to retaliate had contributed to the mistake, my respect for him would ironically have been greatly strengthened. I would add that patients often gain strikingly important understandings of themselves and their analyst after the end of an analysis, when the intensity of the transference and countertransference reactions has waned, allowing surprising, often painful insights and meaningful growth.

One morning, thinking I was to see my next patient an hour later, I was calmly walking out of the office on my way to lunch with a newspaper in hand. The patient, who was in the waiting room, asked, "Am I here at the right time?" Completely taken aback, I clumsily replied "Yes," and went outside, quickly returning to the waiting room pretending I had retrieved something from my car.

After the patient's session, in which the experience in the waiting room was avoided by both of us, I decided to tell the patient when we met the next day that I had lied by acting as though I had not confused the time of her appointment. As I thought about my "mistake," I realized that concerns about an upcoming doctor's appointment and about an ill member of my family contributed to my thinking that I was not scheduled to meet with the patient at that time. However, convinced that there had to be tensions between me and my patient that contributed to my forgetting, I became aware that, recently, I had felt "seduced and dropped" on several occasions by the patient, and understood that I had responded to her in kind. My initial inclination to focus on health concerns was an attempt to protect myself from becoming aware of my resentment and understanding more deeply my vulnerability, as well as the power of my desire to retaliate.

In the following hour, the patient was heatedly detailing things her family did not want to know about her. Not surprisingly, I was virtually certain that this reflected her knowing about my dishonesty and her concern that I did not want to know her reactions to it. Because she believed I did not want her to know about it, and because it would be very painful to know that about me, she did not allow herself to be aware of the fact that I had lied. I noted that she had said nothing about the experience in the waiting room. After a brief pause, the patient said that she remembered my going to my car, but really had no strong reactions to our interaction.

I said that I had not been truthful the previous day and that I was quite certain she knew that but had hidden her knowledge from me as well as from herself. I believed that acknowledging my dishonesty gave her implicit permission to become conscious of what she already knew and to recognize that fears of her intense disappointment and anger, coupled with my vulnerability (I was a sitting duck), need not lead her to blind herself to what she knew. In subsequent sessions, we continued to explore this subject, and, at some point, I said that I understood my forgetting her session was, to some degree, retaliation for experiencing her as very present, followed by a subtle but powerful distancing of herself.

The patient, who had seduced and dropped many men in her life, realized the ways in which she had done that to me. Although this was never made explicit, I believe she also understood that I was vulnerable to feeling distanced. Although embarrassed and ashamed, I believe that the patient's respect for me was strengthened by this experience, even as it required that she acknowledge my dishonesty and incorporate knowledge of my shortcoming. I also think that my dishonesty allowed me to learn something important about myself that contributed to my professional and personal growth. (Note: the patient has read and given permission for this to be published.)

These kinds of actions by the therapist occur when their personal self overrides their professional self (it bears repeating that there is only one, unitary self); or, from a different perspective, when the analyst's countertransference reaction is so strong that they cannot maintain their psychoanalytic balance. The concept of a personal and a professional self is a metaphor for two threads woven into the fabric of the self, a concept that I have found meaningful. Hopefully infrequent, moments when the therapist loses their psychoanalytic balance are inevitable in any meaningful psychotherapy. Personal analysis can reduce, but never eliminate our vulnerabilities.

The manifestations of these vulnerabilities within the psychotherapy provide meaningful opportunities for introspection and change by both therapist and patient. If honestly and professionally managed, they will increase both the patient's respect for the therapist and strengthen the therapist's self-respect. In addition, they provide the therapist with a powerful, immediate experience from which they can learn a great deal about hidden aspects of themselves. By the end of therapy, the patient, in addition to having constructed a much more steadfast and solid self-respect, will have a deep and genuine respect for how successfully the therapist fulfilled the demanding job requirements of being a therapist—requirements that include identifying and owning "mistakes" that are harmful to the patient.

<><><><><><><><><><><><><><><><><><><><><><><><><><><><>

HIDDEN PLEASURE IS THE DEEPEST PAIN STEMMING FROM A SHAMEFUL OR GUILTY ACT.

Shame and guilt powerfully shape a person's sense of themselves and contribute significantly to their caution in allowing themselves to be known and to better know themselves. For some, the emotions are so intense, and the restrictions imposed by them so powerful, that they live as if confined within a prison of shame and/or guilt. The experience of imprisonment foretells the intense relief experienced when they discover that the shame was rooted in childhood experiences (e.g., bed-wetting, masturbation fantasies, etc.) that did not warrant such harsh condemnation and eternal punishment. Or, if the shame was warranted (e.g., cheating on the medical board exam, insider trading, torturing a sibling), that their self-imposed life sentence was overly harsh. Like inmates, the patient may be threatened by freedom, but the common experience of exhilarating liberation reflects the pervasive impact of unconscious imprisonment.

Buried deep beneath the focus on their actions and subsequent remorse lies the patient's searing shame for the satisfaction they experienced while committing them. Only infrequently will a patient give direct voice to this aspect of their shameful actions. More often it falls to the therapist to create an empathic but unflinching way of bringing the patient's satisfaction into focus. This extraordinarily difficult challenge is more readily met when the patient's sadism has become an integral aspect of the therapeutic relationship. A patient who frequently watched movies about the Holocaust had worked with me for many years before their deep satisfaction in torturing me could be brought into our work. Understanding that their guilt and shame were rooted in the satisfaction of causing me pain was extremely meaningful and allowed for the exploration of similar themes within their family.

Some patients who abuse potentially fatal substances or are chronically suicidal gain unspoken satisfaction from keeping those who love them, including the therapist, on edge with the ever-present possibility of an accidental overdose or successful suicide attempt. I have found it important for families and therapists to acknowledge to the patient the constant fear that they force others to endure and to make it clear that, although the anguish will be intense and eternal, those who love and care about them will be able to survive their death. Only if the patient's life means more to them than to their family (and the therapist) do they have a decent chance of overcoming their suicidal urges and addiction.

A therapist who is treating a victim of child sexual abuse has the delicate and extremely difficult task of facilitating a relationship in which the patient can become aware of and acknowledge any excitement they experienced, stimulation that was greatly overshadowed by flooding emotions of terror, shame, guilt, and other feelings. The therapist of a child abuser has the even more challenging task of facilitating a relationship in which the patient can become aware of and discuss the reactions they wanted to induce in the child and the satisfaction they experienced. Even more daunting is the need for the therapist to tolerate the deep revulsion and hatred of the patient's sadism, which will become manifest in some way in the therapeutic relationship. The therapist must be able to metabolize these reactions thoroughly enough to create sufficient empathy for the work to be productive. Needless to say, very few psychotherapists have the personal qualities to accept an abuser as a patient and to work with them effectively.

David I Joseph MD

◇◇

"LINGUISTIC DISAVOWALS" AND GRAMMATICAL "SLIPS OF THE TONGUE" ARE WINDOWS INTO THE UNCONSCIOUS.

I do not recall when I first became aware of what I refer to as "linguistic disavowals," but for many years I have been impressed by their prevalence in everyday discourse. As an English major in college, I learned the importance of paying careful attention to word choice, sentence structure, and the rhythm of writing. Roy Schafer's "action language" (1976) deepened my appreciation of both everyday language and the ways language is used in the clinical relationship. Linguistic disavowal is reflected by the following commonplace statements: "I do not have a relationship with my father"; "She did not participate in class"; "I ended the connection with him."

Linguistic disavowals such as these are so routinely and effortlessly woven into everyday speech that they seldom merit a second thought. Once struck by the obvious contradictions inherent in these and many other commonplace utterances, I understood that commonplace language and unremarkable sentence structure often convey a desire to obscure while simultaneously giving silent expression to unsettling thoughts or painful emotions.

Linguistic disavowals can be meaningfully addressed with patients and are usually responded to with surprisingly ready acceptance and immediate understanding. Transforming linguistic disavowals into an object of analysis provides patients with a compelling glimpse into hidden aspects of themselves. "I do not have a relationship with my father" softens and protects the speaker from the blunt, painful declaration to speaker and listener that "my father was a drunk, violent, abusive bastard whom I hate, am deeply ashamed of, and want nothing to do with." Implicit in this unvarnished, explicit statement is: "and I will always have to live with the sadness and enduring disappointment of never having had the kind of relationship with a father that I continue to yearn for. And, if that weren't enough, I feel guilty for hating him, and wonder what I did that provoked him to treat me so cruelly."

The "data" contained within linguistic disavowal is clear and readily understood by the patient. The choice of language belongs solely to the patient; to the analyst belongs the awareness of its hidden meanings. I was quite concerned that attention to linguistic disavowal would create a more intellectualized therapeutic conversation, but my experience has been quite the opposite. When their language becomes the object of analysis, I have been surprised how readily patients understand that their unconscious word choice and sentence structure has been used to empty their speech of intense, distressing thoughts and affects. Linguistic disavowal is often manifest in the ways patients give voice to their experience of the therapist. "Therapy has been really helpful," dilutes the intimate relationship that is the essence of psychotherapy. "You have really been helpful to me" more accurately reflects the emotional depth of the relationship.

This intimacy impacts therapists, too, frequently leading them to refer to "the therapy." Such expressions give patient and therapist a breather from an obsessive, potentially suffocating focus on the relationship. Exploring unconscious thoughts and emotions that are conveyed linguistically needs to be done with the same tact (Poland 1975), attention to timing, and tone as any other intervention that draws patients' attention to unsettling, hidden aspects of themselves. Language may seem intrinsically different from other adaptive actions which a patient uses to manage internal threats and discomfort, but making language an object of analysis requires no less care than any other interpretive intervention.

How frequently do therapists hear a patient say, "This is not a real relationship." Although such a declaration understands "unreal" to be a synonym for "artificial," it unconsciously gives voice to a number of unsettling concerns. Conceptualizing the relationship with their therapists as unreal allows patients to dilute, if not deny entirely, the all too meaningful intimacy, all too intense rivalry, all too exciting sexual fantasies and terrifying fears, about themselves and their therapist. Viewing the relationship as unreal often reflects the patient's reactions to the painful reality that the relationship began and continues because they are renting the therapist's time and purchasing the therapist's expertise.

Both patient and therapist know that, were there no financial aspect to their relationship, their meetings would end. Underneath this self-evident reality may lie the patient's concern that their nastiness, competitiveness, repulsiveness, deep yearning, and intense loving are so repugnant, threatening, and insatiable that, were it not for the regular payment of a fee, the therapist would never enter into, much less remain, in a meaningful relationship with them. Or, if the relationship is "not real," then neither is the patient's disappointment at the ways in which the relationship is limited.

A corollary of "this is not a real relationship" is the artificial distinction between the "real" relationship and the "transference" relationship. There is only one relationship, developed over years of difficult, challenging work. We may conceptualize and speak of the "real" and the "transferential" aspects of the relationship as though they were separate, but there is only one relationship, just as there is only a single self.

Common difficulties motivating patients to seek treatment include an explosion of anger, an unrestrained buying spree, or some other behavior that seems out of character. This is often expressed and experienced as a "loss of control," and patients frequently give voice to fears of "losing control." The patient speaks as though they are afraid of having an epileptic seizure. Or they may describe their explosions of temper as though they were driving, stepped on the brake, and found that the pedal went straight to the floor. Others evoke the image of a dam suddenly breaking with a wild, violent torrent of pent-up fury, or nonchalantly describe having "lost control" as though they had lost the keys to their house.

Such linguistic constructions powerfully deny the patient's intense, terrifying struggle. They are caught between their wish to soften the intensity and contain the expression of their emotions and their unconscious desire to relax or even relinquish control entirely. Although often unconscious, relinquishing control can be quite satisfying. Exploding, sobbing, spending too much money, or immersing oneself in a forbidden sexual relationship gives rise to more than anxiety, shame, and guilt. By experiencing these actions as a loss of control, the patient disavows desire and agency as well as guilt and shame. "I lost control" drains all responsibilty from "I didn't control myself" or "I didn't want to be so controlled." How best to help the patient to become aware of these desires will vary, but listening for linguistic disavowals will facilitate awareness of the patient's creatively hidden desires.

Many psychoanalysts seem concerned that breaking a generally accepted precedent will put them on a "slippery slope," as though their psychoanalytic automobile has hit an unseen patch of black ice, and the analyst-driver cannot stop or control its direction. Flexibility can be misused in the service of proving to oneself and the patient that one is a "good object" and disproving that one is a "bad object," but fears of putting oneself on a slippery slope reflects the analyst's fears of their own desires to have a less restricted relationship with the patient. Laws are meant to achieve justice, and, when following the law would lead to an unjust action, the ethical choice is to break the law. So, too, with the "laws" of good psychoanalytic practice. They are standards that should only be employed when they will further the therapeutic work.

"After one or two drinks you really have a tough time limiting how much more you can tolerate," Mr. M. said, explaining his long-standing alcohol misuse. "You really only have control over the first one." Although quite unaware of it, Mr. M. was expressing his wish that I, too, had experienced similar struggles with alcohol. If true, my personal experience would allow me to be better able to help him refrain from taking an initial drink, to know what an intense, constant struggle he wages with himself, and to respond empathically when he satisfies his craving for alcohol. In addition, if I have difficulty controlling my use of alcohol, I will be less likely to lose respect for him and will not draw a bead on his shame and guilt.

"It is difficult to discuss, but I want to talk about sex with you," said Ms. Jacobs, a 35-year-old divorced mother of two who had been working with me for several years. Clearly, she intended to say, "It is difficult to discuss but I want to talk with you about sex," but had unconsciously structured her words to make it clear that her desire for a sexual relationship with me was intense and creating considerable distress. Her wording also makes it abundantly clear that talking candidly with me about her sexual feelings was going to be extremely difficult. Had she structured her sentence the way she consciously wanted, her sexual fantasies about me would have been much more hidden. The clarity of her declaration does not indicate that this was the moment to draw her attention to her feelings about me. In fact, her unconscious sentence construction would suggest that such a discussion would be premature. However, had I been unaware of the unconscious intent of her sentence, I would have engaged in a "missed understanding" and might have avoided addressing it entirely. If that had occurred, I believe Ms. Jacobs would unconsciously have believed that I was so threatened by her desire that I did not allow myself to experience it.

"The panic returned."

"The depression lifted."

Commonplace statements like these convey the patient's sense that their mental experience, both thought and affect, is caused by some external agent, an experience over which they have neither responsibility nor control. "I was able to concentrate better today" subtly but meaningfully asserts one's active participation and agency, while "my concentration was better," relinquishes it. When patients believe they lack agency over the creation of their thoughts and feelings, they internalize the belief that their depressed or irritable mood can only be ameliorated by something outside themselves. Unlike adults, adolescents are developmentally conflicted about assuming responsibility for their own behavior (Chused 1988), a state of mind that is often camouflaged by their apparent maturity.

It is important for patients to understand that, despite genetic and constitutional predispositions to anxiety, depression, and other mental states, they can reduce their vulnerability to negative stimuli and learn adaptive strategies to manage symptoms effectively. Individuals who reject or struggle to understand this may be unconsciously motivated by shame, guilt, or other concerns, but creating a different perspective allows the patient to develop greater control and agency, regardless of any inborn predisposition. This is true even for individuals with manic-depressive disorder and schizophrenic disorders who, once they understand the kinds of stimuli that are especially impactful, can learn to identify and respond to these experiences in ways that may allow them to avoid cognitive and emotional disorganization.

EVERYDAY LANGUAGE IS OFTEN MISLEADING

While everyday conversation may involve careful attention to word choice and sentence structure, for the most part we use language and organize our speech without much "thought." This "everyday," unremarkable language and speech often provides a window into unconscious thought and emotion.

SELF-DISCIPLINE.

The development of self-discipline is a complex process that evolves throughout a lifetime. One can consider self-discipline from several perspectives. Among them is the impact of internalized object relationships with the "disciplinarians" of one's childhood and adolescence. Since the exercise of self-discipline may be unconsciously experienced as being disciplined by an internalized object who imposes unwarranted and unwanted discipline upon us, self-discipline is an unending challenge.

This unconscious process elicits a range of responses, including submission, dominance, rebellion, control, and resentment, and provides deeper understanding why diets, exercise regimens, and New Year's Resolutions are so difficult to sustain. The dieter's craving for a delectable piece of lemon meringue pie reflects the desire to savor the taste of the pie, but it also grows out of the profound satisfaction that comes with throwing off the yoke of an unrelenting, rigid, internalized disciplinarian. Self-indulgence is a very well-camouflaged breakout from a prison sentence "unfairly" imposed by an unconscious other. A patient's experience that they must be on time, use the couch, give voice to whatever comes to mind, never ask a personal question or challenge other "rules" reflects the powerful impact of an internalized disciplinarian.

<><><><><><><><><><><><><><><><><><><><><><><><><><><><>

SEPARATION ANXIETY AND SEPARATION-INDIVIDUATION.

Mahler's (Mahler, M., Pine, F., and Bergman, A. 1975) seminal work explored the experience of infants who imperceptibly and inexorably develops an awareness of themselves and their mother as two individuals, once completely immersed in each other, but increasingly experiencing their own separateness. She hypothesized that the child responds to this individuation with apprehension, with "separation anxiety," a concept that continues to be central to our understanding of child development. The concept of separation anxiety is a very mature way of understanding what I imagine the very young child experiences. "Separation-individuation" suggests, at least for me, the division of an amoeba into two separate cells, separate but genetically indistinguishable. Melanie Klein believed that the young child experienced the mother as nurturing or depriving, with the sense of being deprived evolving into an experience of being attacked. Regardless of how the child's mental experience has been conceptualized, in the earliest months of life, it is unformulated (Stern 1983).

In contrast, I imagine that the child gradually comes to experience the mother as either present or absent, holding or abandoning, nurturing or withholding, gratifying or disappointing, soothing or irritating, loving or frightening. Although I have used these evocative words, I believe that the very young infant experiences only their unformulated forerunners. The topic of aloneness and solitude has been extensively explored by Quinodoz (Quinodoz, J-M 1993) and the subject of "separation-individuation" has recently been reconsidered in two very thoughtful articles (Kanwal 2023) (Stern 2023) that are consistent with my understanding of the experience of the developing child.

From this perspective, the experience of separateness is a consequence of repeatedly feeling abandoned by and abandoning the mother, and separation anxiety is the anxiety precipitated by fear of being permanently abandoned by and/or abandoning her. From this perspective, the infant and very young child experience "abandonment anxiety" rather than separation anxiety. The experience of becoming an individual, separate from the mother, embodies both a freedom from and a continuing longing for the lost experience of feeling completely immersed in her. "Separating" suggests a smooth, constant process that is ultimately complete, but the lifelong development of the mother-child relationship, however it is conceptualized, is not always smooth and never truly complete.

Abandonment anxiety often contains intense reactions to many situations other than being left or leaving the mother. Going to school may be extremely stressful, not so much because the child misses or feels guilty about leaving the mother, but because they cannot tolerate the fact that their younger siblings have mother all to themselves. Going to college may elicit intense self-doubt about one's academic ability or painful homesickness, which may mask fears about how one will manage the freedom to indulge in drugs, sex, and rock and roll.

A middle-aged man sought consultation because his job required frequent travel, during which he experienced extreme anxiety and sadness, echoing the difficulties he experienced as a child when he dreaded going to camp, a pattern repeated during college. He believed that the anguish he felt while travelling was a continuation of these childhood experiences. It was only after considerable psychotherapy that he came to realize that he was terrified of the powerful sexual temptations he felt while on the road, and that his underlying concern about being at camp and at college had been his attraction to his classmates.

~∞∞∞∞∞∞∞∞∞∞∞∞∞∞∞∞∞∞∞∞∞∞∞∞∞∞∞∞∞∞∞~

DEPENDENCE AND INDEPENDENCE.

These concepts are frequently characterized as binary states of mind, and human development is often conceptualized as involving the gradual evolution of the dependence/independence ratio, with the child ultimately achieving "independence" and adulthood. This binary concept implies that "dependence" in adulthood reflects immaturity, an uncompleted psychological development. At first blush, independence may seem synonymous with maturity, but linguistically, it minimizes or denies that we are, need, and sometimes wish to be dependent on many different individuals to meet a range of psychological and physical needs throughout our lives.

A patient whose awareness of feeling dependent on me is mixed with considerable apprehension and shame communicates an anxiety-filled recognition of my profound importance to them. Yet, the specific ways in which they feel dependent—what they need me to give them—cannot be assumed and requires careful exploration. Patients may depend on me as someone to spar, compete, and not infrequently fight with, or someone to admire and sexually desire them. The ways in which our patients depend on us are multiple.

The corollary of this perspective is that the goal of a child's development is not independence but autonomy, an autonomy that includes the ability to recognize, own, and respect one's multiple dependencies throughout life, and be comfortable seeking to have them met.

◇◇◇

SELFLESSNESS AND SELF-SACRIFICE.

Selflessness and self-sacrifice are oxymorons. Although one might wish to be selfless and self-sacrificing, the desire is simply incapable of being fulfilled. Every action is motivated by a desire to gratify some aspect of the self. Mother Teresa may well have considered herself to be acting completely without self-interest, devoting her entire being to supporting and assisting the desperately poor and unimaginably deprived citizens of Calcutta. She was universally admired and beatified for her sacrifices.

However, whether consciously or not, she sought and achieved deep meaning and abiding satisfaction from sacrificing the gratification of nearly all her desires to achieve the pleasure that grew from attending so admirably to the welfare of the poor. Privately and perhaps unconsciously, she may have derived pleasure and a sense of moral superiority from her many sacrifices. Regardless, she created a life that provided fulfillment and meaning to an essential aspect of her self. Selfless she was most certainly not.

Many examples of "selflessness" and "self-sacrifice" are routinely encountered in our daily lives, personal and professional. The father who laments, sometimes bitterly, the golf games he has turned down "for the welfare of the children" denies that he chooses to forego golf to be the good father he aspires to be and to develop a satisfying relationship with his children. He chooses to sacrifice the pleasure of golf, but in no way is he self-sacrificing. Mothers who forego graduate school until their youngest child has begun their formal education may struggle with similar experiences of self-sacrifice. In these situations, one frequently encounters a lack of awareness regarding the self-gratification inherent in these actions. Belief in self-sacrifice can insidiously nurture a sense of moral martyrdom, deep resentment, or corrosive bitterness toward those for whom one has "sacrificed."

LOW SELF-ESTEEM AND LACK OF SELF-CONFIDENCE.

Low self-esteem and lack of self-confidence suggest a failure to achieve enough meaningful accomplishments to foster an enduring sense of satisfaction and self-respect. The individual thinks and feels that their reservoir of admirable qualities and confidence in their abilities is nowhere near full. From this perspective, the problem primarily lies in the patient falling short of some personal goals and/or relentlessly devaluing their accomplishments. Often, however, the patient's devaluation of themselves results not so much from a meager storehouse of positive feelings about themselves, but from the unconscious knowledge of a shameful, guilt-infused sense of self. This aspect of the patient is so powerful as to render relatively meaningless any positive sense of themselves.

For such a person, understanding their difficulty as lacking "enough" self-esteem is much less painful than being aware of a pervasive sense of shame, unworthiness, or guilt. The patient fears that these aspects of their character will totally overwhelm their sense of personal goodness.

Adopted children who feel that they are not good enough may struggle with an unconscious sense of "badness," rooted in the unconscious conviction that disgusting, unlovable aspects of themselves led their mothers and fathers to give them away. In their treatment, they often fear that they will offend or hurt the therapist who will also send them away. For others, the sense of badness may stem from the death or sadistic treatment of a sibling, distressing shame about one's denied sexual orientation, intense hatred of one or both parents, or the consequences of physical or sexual abuse.

Individuals with a physical defect such as the absence of a finger may create a defective sense of self that perfuses their experience. Many psychological dynamics can contribute to a private, unconscious conviction of personal badness, but patients who suffer from low self-esteem may use this concept to shield themselves from awareness of their defective self-concept.

The focus on not having enough "goodness" protects both patient and therapist from encountering too much of the patient's badness. No admirable accomplishments and no number of accolades can neutralize a conviction of personal unworthiness. When a sense of unworthiness is pervasive and deeply rooted, the individual's conviction may lead them to limit or devalue their accomplishments, thereby reinforcing their unworthiness and inflicting upon themselves the unhappiness they feel they deserve. This dynamic is a variant of Freud's (1916) description of individuals whose criminal motivation stems from a reservoir of unconscious guilt.

A woman in her late 20s became extremely depressed in college and was treated with an anti-depressant but did not receive meaningful psychotherapy. Always a star in her girls' high school, especially in math and science where the answers were always right and wrong, in college she became increasingly burdened by crippling doubt about her capabilities. She was especially terrified to share her ideas in classes such as literature and history where there were no correct answers. Flooded with anxiety, sadness, and insecurity, she sought therapy, tearfully saying that she had completely "lost her self-confidence."

As her psychoanalytic psychotherapy progressed, she gradually became aware of her hidden shame and deep humiliation whenever she was "wrong" or disagreed with the opinions of others. The intensity of her shame reflected other, unconscious aspects of herself that were infused with unworthiness, especially her intense jealousy of a younger sister whom she had sometimes tormented unmercifully. To avoid the possibility of being "wrong," she isolated herself and became flooded with a "lack of confidence."

As she became aware of her shame, guilt, and fear of her resentment and rivalry, she gradually understood that she did not lack self-confidence. Rather, these emotions rendered her unworthy of any success, admiration, or recognition. She was also frightened that she might use her intellect, competence, and power hurtfully. As the therapy progressed, she also came to understand that, given her relationship with her sister, she feared "deliberately" humiliating herself as a way of incurring the punishment she believed she deserved.

Reframing is sometimes understood as belonging in the purview of cognitive/behavioral psychotherapies and seen as antithetical to psychoanalytic psychotherapy. Reframing in cognitive/behavioral therapies helps the patient develop a different perspective by redefining the experience. "Just because you got a B doesn't mean you are a failure." Reframing in psychoanalysis occurs by helping the patient become aware of unconscious motivations that resulted in their harsh judgment.

<<<><><><><><><><><><><><><><><><><><><><><><><><><>>>

EMPTINESS AND DEADNESS.

The uniquely painful experience of emptiness and deadness silently and powerfully conveys wordless despair and profound hopelessness. Although suffused with suffering, a patient's experience of emptiness and deadness overlays thoughts and feelings they cannot allow themselves to know, bear, or share with another. Concern about their ability to bear the burden of this anguish is often accompanied by the conviction that no one can, or wishes to, witness their suffering and help them metabolize it (Poland 2000). Emptiness and deadness are harrowing, sorrowful experiences, but they are better tolerated than the unrelenting anguish and despair that spring from an unconscious experience of an aliveness that is filled with hatred, shame, and guilt. Better to feel dead that endure such a painful aliveness.

The patient may be convinced that the therapist, too, dreads experiencing these emotions with them. The aliveness is too filled with the experience of abandonment, rejection, or failure to be tolerated, and the emptiness too replete with anger, burning shame and haunting guilt to be known or shared. How striking it is that the experience of deadness and emptiness are often misunderstood, not recognized as manifestations of a state of mind all too alive, all too filled with agony and dread.

INHUMAN, ANIMALISTIC, MONSTROUS....

Common language is used in a myriad of ways to deny those aspects of human behavior that we find repugnant, horrifying, violent, and devoid of concern for the other. We have created and unquestionably incorporated this language because, deep within us, we know that these behaviors are all too human. Such aspects of being human are unremarkable, common qualities of childhood, but we rarely, if ever, refer to a child as inhuman or monstrous. Only when these aspects of our humanity are reflected in the actions of adults do we use words to strip them of any resonance with our unconscious childhood selves.

A related process of disavowal is reflected in other, common language. At first blush, a phrase such as "I am not myself," is simply another way of expressing that one is in a state of mind that contrasts sharply, usually distressingly, with one's usual sense of self. Woven within the phrase, however, is the wish that a particular state of mind, such as deep sadness or unsettling irritability, although experienced infrequently, is not an integral aspect of oneself. Similarly, a patient who expresses concern that he is not masculine enough is using language to camouflage the dread that he is too feminine. Since these words and phrases are so commonplace, the denial is more likely to be unrecognized by both patient and therapist.

◇◇◇◇◇◇◇◇◇◇◇◇◇◇◇◇◇◇◇◇◇◇◇◇◇◇◇◇◇◇◇

POWER DOES NOT CORRUPT.

Often sought and desired, power, like agency, is frequently feared and avoided. John Emerich Edward Dalberg Acton (1834–1902) penned the worn-out phrase: "Power tends to corrupt, and absolute power corrupts absolutely." Rarely cited is his concluding observation: "Great men are almost always bad men." Captured in Acton's declaration is the significant impact of power on its possessor—an inexorable, relentless temptation to use that power to dominate, exploit, aggrandize, acquire, achieve revenge, and conquer sexually.

Power, however, does not corrupt. Power is used corruptly by "bad men," by men whose self-discipline is weakened by the seductive lure of using power destructively. In Acton's mind, greatness is usually associated with badness, but, even if that is true, power does not generate "bad" actions. "Bad" desires lead to bad actions, especially if the individual has power. Power is often used to accomplish good, but the fear of possessing and misusing it has a profound impact on many individuals. Well intentioned hopes of "empowering" patients commonly fall victim to the patient's unconscious terror of becoming empowered, a dread that possessing it will lead them to weaponize it and direct it destructively toward people they hate and love, including the therapist.

Powerlessness is also neutral. If one trusts the person who has power, as when undergoing anesthesia and surgery, powerlessness leads to a desired outcome. However, for individuals with a strong persecutory inclination, being anesthetized and completely at the mercy of the surgeon can be terrifying. This persecutory concern may also reflect unconscious pleasures—sexual and otherwise—in being hurt, a projection of their own sadism or terror carried over from experiences of physical or sexual abuse as a child.

The common and frequently fierce battle against being or feeling controlled reflects a similar concern. Fear of being controlled can be observed in many mundane behaviors, such as the relentless back-seat driver. In the absence of persecutory concerns, putting oneself completely in the hands of another who has earned one's trust, be they surgeon, dentist, or airline pilot, elicits a sense of being well cared for.

In any meaningful psychoanalytic psychotherapy, the therapist can expect to be frightened by the power of transference and countertransference reactions which, while deeply unsettling, need to be tolerated, understood, and explored empathically and tactfully. As a supervisor I have often thought that therapists who have significant difficulty becoming aware of, understanding, and addressing transference reactions in their work are extremely apprehensive of experiencing the intensity and full range of the patient's feelings about them. They seem to fear both the power that patients attribute to them and the actual influence they, as therapists, possess.

It is tempting for therapists to respond quickly to intense transference reactions by interpreting them in the context of the patient's childhood experiences. While such interventions may be accurate and meaningful, they momentarily direct attention away from the psychotherapeutic relationship, the patient's deep feelings about the therapist, the therapist's awareness of their own power, and their fear of how they will use it.

◇◇◇◇◇◇◇◇◇◇◇◇◇◇◇◇◇◇◇◇◇◇◇◇◇◇◇◇◇◇◇◇◇◇◇◇◇◇◇

SELF-ANALYSIS IS AN OXYMORON.

In his characteristically incisive style, Poland (1984) discusses how the closest we come to addressing the "question of neutrality in a self-analysis ... is the countertransference, though, in deference to Freud and in candor to ourselves, I suggest the primary problem in self-analysis is that of case selection." True enough, but "self-analysis," the very phrase, is subtly misleading, implying, through its very name, an omnipotent belief that one can experience an analysis without an analyst. Linguistic nit-picking by a language-obsessed psychoanalyst? Perhaps, since it is obvious that self-analysis is a synonym for analytically informed introspection. However, I would suggest that self-analysis expresses a wish masquerading as a belief that undertaking a thorough, rigorous analytic self-examination, or even conducting an honest, creatively imagined conversation with one's former analyst, can fully counter the power and influence of one's unconscious avoidance of deeply unsettling private experience. Lakoff and Johnson (1999, 233) have noted that the development of self-understanding:

> ... is not unlike other forms of understanding—it comes out of our constant interactions with our physical, cultural, and interpersonal environment. At a minimum the skills for achieving MUTUAL understanding are necessary even to approach SELF-understanding.... Self-understanding requires unending negotiation and re-negotiation of the meaning of your experiences to yourself. In therapy ... much

of self-understanding involves consciously recognizing previously unconscious metaphors and how you live by them.
It involves the constant construction of new coherences in
your life, coherences that give new meaning to old experiences. The process of self-understanding is the continual
development of new life stories for yourself.

Lakoff and Johnson's perspective on the development of self-
understanding, in my view, does not convey sufficient respect
for the powerful, relentless unconscious determination to avoid
acknowledging and owning unsettling, aggressive, shameful, and
guilt-ridden aspects of ourselves—a determination that may be
diminished but never entirely eliminated even through the most
transformative psychoanalysis. The ongoing process of an honest, rigorous, thorough, psychoanalytically informed process of
introspection is essential for any psychoanalytic psychotherapist,
but it is not self-analysis. Conceptualizing it as such devalues
the power of our unconscious and insulates us from grieving the
absence of our analyst. Our unconscious is simply too relentless,
too insistent, too powerful to be neutralized.

The term "self-analysis" suggests the ever-present, irreconcil-
able desires for oneness and twoness, immersion and emersion,
for the togetherness and aloneness that characterize all loving
relationships and are a central focus within any psychoanalysis. It
also evokes, for anyone who has experienced a meaningful psychoanalytic treatment, the enduring sorrow at the loss of their analyst.

PRACTICAL SOLUTIONS FOR AWKWARD SITUATIONS IN CLINICAL PRACTICE

Awkward, embarrassing clinical moments are unavoidable, commonly experienced, and not explored often enough. What follows is an all-too-brief exploration of some of the conundrums with which I have wrestled. Each experience was uncomfortable—some were infused with shame and regret. Each also created an opportunity for meaningful psychotherapeutic work.

◇◇

HOW TO ADDRESS A PATIENT; HOW TO BE ADDRESSED ONESELF.

What name to use when addressing a patient or what name to ask that the patient use when speaking to the therapist are questions that may well be uncomfortable for both parties. In actual practice, I rarely use a patient's name during a session, and patients rarely use mine. When I telephone a patient, if the patient answers, I say "this is Dr. Joseph," although in this era of cell phones and caller ID, the patient usually knows I am calling. If another family member answers, I ask if "Robert Mattis" is there.

If a patient wishes to call me by my first name, I initially explore why they prefer that way of addressing me. After reaching some understanding of the patient's preference, I will explain that psychoanalysis is both very personal and very professional and that, in my experience, being on a first name basis implicitly deemphasizes the professional aspect of our relationship and has a negative effect on the therapy. Except when working with adolescents, I never address a patient by their first name while expecting that they address me as Dr. Joseph. I believe that such a custom would establish a hierarchical relationship which would be harmful to the therapy.

On the few occasions when I have worked with someone whom I have known casually, first names seem most natural. Attempting to underscore the professional dimension of our relationship by using formal names would have felt artificial, but in these situations, one has to be constantly alert to the temptation of both patient and therapist to exploit social familiarity to avoid the most difficult topics, especially those that pertain to the therapeutic relationship. While some therapists (I was told that Roy Schafer did this) use first names toward the end of the therapy, I have been concerned that moving to a "first name basis" might dilute the very painful work of ending the therapy.

<><><><><><><><><><><><><><><><><><><><><><><><><><><><>

WHEN TO INTRODUCE AN ADMINISTRATIVE ISSUE.

Deciding when to introduce administrative matters, such as schedule changes, session cancellations, or vacation dates, is a routine, mildly awkward situation. Introducing the subject at the beginning of a session shapes the flow of the session, an impact that is especially unfortunate if the patient comes to the session in considerable distress. Introducing a change in the middle of the session interrupts the ongoing conversation. Announcing the change at the end of the hour does not give the patient any time to respond to the issue, leaving them to wrestle with their reactions until the next session.

I have known therapists who prefer each of the above, but, unless the patient is clearly distraught, I prefer to introduce all administrative matters at the outset of a session. This ensures ample time to explore the patient's reaction to the change. More importantly, informing the patient of the matter at the beginning frees me from the necessity of remembering to raise the issue before the session ends, a preoccupation that interferes significantly with my ability to listen associatively and to develop a state of reverie.

FORGETTING AN APPOINTMENT AND DISCOVERING TWO PATIENTS IN THE WAITING ROOM.

Although I am very much a creature of habit, I always assume that forgetting a patient's appointment is, to some degree, the product of my countertransference reaction. If I can achieve an understanding of my forgetting, the patient and I can explore it productively. If I cannot achieve an understanding, we have to live with the uncertainty, a situation in which the patient has to absorb being injured by me, and I have to live with my disappointment, regret, and shame.

The shock of walking into the waiting room and discovering two patients waiting for me with obvious but unspoken discomfort is awkward and embarrassing, a situation greatly aggravated if one shares an office and there are other patients in the waiting room. Sometimes, one patient will realize they have made a mistake, but often the fault has been mine. When I have scheduled two people for the same time, it has usually resulted from my having made an appointment when I am at home and do not have my appointment book with me (a generational confession: I still use a paper calendar). However, even when that is the obvious explanation, I always assume that something out of my awareness has contributed to my confusion.

Choosing which person to see is a lose-lose-lose situation. All three individuals will be powerfully impacted, and, although everyone may wish to minimize it, the fallout may be significant. When I have forgotten an appointment or have double booked, I do not charge the patient for their next session. I believe that their time is as valuable as mine, and I do not consider this position to be the product of excessive guilt, although I do have a personal storehouse to contend with. One consequence of not charging for the next appointment is that the patient may use my policy to blunt their pain and anger.

<><><><><><><><><><><><><><><><><><><><><><><><><>

FALLING ASLEEP.

Every therapist has the nightmare of falling asleep while listening to a patient, an experience that is humiliating for the therapist and painful for the patient. When talking to a patient face to face, the therapist is caught dead to rights. Patients become aware the very moment we start to doze, and, while a friend told me that one of his patients waited 20 minutes for the end of her hour, saying nothing and exiting quietly, my patients have awakened me in a flash. When talking with patients who are using the couch, denial is always an option—a lousy one, but an option nonetheless. It is a lousy option because I believe patients know that we are lying and ashamed.

When I have fallen asleep while listening to a patient who is lying on the couch and have awakened before the patient asks "Are you sleeping?" I faced a different dilemma. I believe that, on some level, the patient knows I have dozed, even if only for a few seconds, and therefore the better choice is to ask if they were aware that I nodded off. Most often that is the choice I make, but I have not always found the courage to do so. When speaking with patients who are using a chair, I create a different problem by sometimes closing my eyes to create a state of mind that, for me, facilitates psychoanalytic listening. When I close my eyes, regardless of how alert I am, I raise the patient's concern that I have fallen asleep. But, since I often listen more productively with my eyes closed, I have explained why I do this and acknowledge that it may make them uncomfortable.

To protect the therapist who has fallen asleep from their hurt and anger, many patients are quick to blame themselves for being boring, repetitive, or uninteresting. I have not fallen asleep often, but when I have, it has usually been during sessions where something is being consciously withheld or unconsciously avoided. In these situations, the alertness that usually characterizes my listening wanes imperceptibly. Sometimes I sense it early enough to avoid dozing, and can indicate to the patient that I am getting sleepy, wondering aloud what may be going on between us that is contributing to it.

CONFUSING ONE PATIENT'S HISTORY WITH ANOTHER'S.

I confuse patients' histories so rarely that I am shocked when a patient informs me that I must be confusing them with someone else. Upon reflection, I usually can identify the confusion and may even arrive at some understanding about what stimulated me to make the error. Patients respond to their hurt in a variety of ways, but always leave the experience with heightened concerns that they are not very important to me, are very forgettable, or, most painful, are so irritating and difficult that I would like to get rid of them. If I can determine some dynamic between the patient and me that has contributed to my confusion, I will offer it for our exploration, but that is not always possible. Thankfully, my sample size is small, something I attribute to the unique qualities of psychoanalytic listening, not to my extraordinary memory.

◇◇

THE PATIENT IS INTOXICATED.

How best to respond when a patient comes to a session intoxicated with alcohol or any other substance is a question that I initially found difficult to answer. I have always thought that talking with an intoxicated person does not lead to meaningful learning. After some years of practice, this conviction allowed me to explain my thinking and policy without feeling that I have shamed the patient. The first time the patient arrives under the influence, I tell them that, in the future, I won't meet with them if they are intoxicated, explaining that I do not think our conversation will be productive.

◇◇◇◇◇◇◇◇◇◇◇◇◇◇◇◇◇◇◇◇◇◇◇◇◇◇◇◇◇◇◇◇◇◇◇

A PATIENT DRESSES AND ACTS SEDUCTIVELY.

When they experience a patient dressing and acting seductively, many psychotherapists are extremely uncomfortable. If they are aroused, their discomfort is infinitely greater. Uncomfortable, embarrassed if aroused, worried about turning up the heat, concerned that the patient will feel chastised, and finding themselves at a loss for words, therapists may not address the issue at all. The patient, finding their seductiveness ignored, may up the ante in subsequent sessions or may correctly conclude that the therapist is so uncomfortable with being the object of their desire that the prudent choice is to banish sexuality from the consulting room. Seductiveness ought not be more surprising than sadness, competition, jealousy, resentment, fury, or any other state of mind.

If the patient is professionally dressed but acting seductively, I have found it useful to say something like "I sense that you are feeling seductive today." If the patient is dressed seductively, I note how they dressed and inquire about what motivated their clothing selection. It is noteworthy to me that therapists are much more concerned about the risk of sexual "boundary violations" than aggressive boundary violations. Sexual relationships between patient and therapist are not rare, but I have never heard of a patient and therapist getting into a physical fight.

<><><><><><><><><><><><><><><><><><><><><><><><><><><><>

PATIENTS WHO EXPOSE THEMSELVES.

A man who sits with his legs draped over an arm of the chair or a woman in a short skirt lounging on the chair with her legs spread apart, both exposing their genitalia, create an extremely uncomfortable dilemma for the therapist. The therapist is invited to look and yet feels compelled not to look. If they look, they are a voyeur; if they do not look, they act as if they are frightened by what they have seen or have been rendered blind by extreme discomfort. Embarrassed and ashamed, wishing that the behavior was not "intentional," therapists often freeze, hoping that the patient will shift their position and never repeat the behavior. Not only is that unlikely to occur, but, if the therapist does not find a way to bring the behavior into the therapy, the patient will, at some level, perceive the therapist's extreme discomfort. The lack of acknowledgment will prevent the exposure from becoming part of the therapy, and the patient will feel increased shame and fear of the power of their sexual desires. The interaction will become a variant of a "missed understanding."

In such circumstances, I have found it most comfortable for myself and the patient to say, "Are you aware that you are exposing yourself?" While the patient may be embarrassed, regardless of whether they are aware of their behavior, the therapist has tactfully and respectfully integrated the patient's behavior into the treatment process, doing so in a manner that is neither shaming nor presuming to know the patient's conscious or unconscious motivation.

The simple question, "Are you aware?" minimizes

embarrassment while drawing attention to something the patient needs to know and to explore with the therapist. Similarly, "Are you aware that your blouse is unbuttoned?" and "Are you aware that your fly is unzipped?" are tactful interventions. "Are you aware" is a helpful intervention in many delibidinized moments.

"Are you aware that you are consistently five minutes late for our sessions?"

"Are you aware that you do not close the door when you leave?"

"Are you aware …" is an intervention that makes the patient's behavior an object of analysis without presuming to understand its meaning.

◇◇

INVITATIONS AND OTHER SOCIAL SITUATIONS.

In smaller cities, therapists have considerable knowledge of and contact with patients outside the confines of the office, but in any location, patients and therapists may be invited to the same event. Some therapists believe strongly that any interaction with a patient outside the office, personal or professional, is detrimental to the therapy. Therefore, when invited to any event, be it a wedding or a dinner party, they ask for the guest list, declining the invitation if a patient has been invited. While this avoids knowingly socializing with a patient, declining an invitation after reviewing the guest list compromises the patient's confidentiality. The host knows that one of the invitees is a patient. Other therapists ask for the guest list and, if a patient is included, will discuss the matter with the patient before deciding whether one or both of them will attend. Every therapist will develop some system to manage these common dilemmas. While social interactions with patients certainly impact the therapeutic relationship, I do not believe that they are simply hurtful. However, if they are not thoroughly explored, the therapy and the patient will be damaged.

When encountering a patient at a movie or restaurant, I always allow the patient to decide whether to acknowledge me. If, by chance, I am seated next to a patient at a restaurant, I will ask to have my table changed.

◇◇

KNOWING SOMEONE WHO IS CLOSE TO THE PATIENT.

This problem is unavoidable in psychoanalytic institutes where teachers, supervisors, and analysts know each other well and may be close friends, and where classmates may have the same analyst. Because I work in a large city with many therapists I deeply respect, when a current patient refers a close friend for treatment, I do not accept the referral. Among other difficulties, for friends to share a therapist unavoidably raises difficult issues of confidentiality. One of my supervisors found himself treating two people who turned out to be close friends, both of whom soon discovered they were seeing the same analyst. After being bombarded repeatedly by one with information about the other, he addressed the problem by deciding to share everything one person said about the other. That struck me then as a unique solution, although not one with which I was entirely comfortable. It did, however, reflect the challenge created by such situations.

Therapists cannot avoid learning about friends, public figures, and other patients, and every therapist tries heroically to compartmentalize the information. It is especially surprising that therapists often act as though compartmentalization actually prevents the information from impacting their minds. That belief is pure fantasy, a myth embraced to ease the tension of their work. Child psychiatrists routinely use compartmentalization to keep information confidential between children and their parents. But, while therapists can choose not to share the child's information with the parents, they cannot keep it confidential from themselves. The information shared in confidence influences how they relate and listen to the parents and the child each time they meet with them.

The same dilemma faces a therapist who sees a patient in both individual and group psychotherapy, or a couple therapist who meets separately with each member of the couple. I have done very little family and group psychotherapy, but, because I think compartmentalization is an illusion and that everything told to me in private will be reflected, one way or another, in all my clinical work with the patient, I will not meet individually with members of a couple or members of a group. I have found it very important to remind myself repeatedly that my "successes" at compartmentalization are only wishful thinking.

◇◇

WHEN THE THERAPIST CRIES, LOSES THEIR TEMPER, OR IS AROUSED.

I have heard both experienced and less experienced psychotherapists describe with shame that they were moved to tears by a patient relating a very sad event. Often, they have tried to hide their crying. The therapist's shame implies that a "well-analyzed" therapist would not be so profoundly impacted by the patient, and their empathy would not elicit tears. Each therapist has their own threshold for experiencing and expressing the full range of affects. In my opinion, if a therapist never loses their affective balance, I would be concerned that the relationship between patient and therapist was characterized by too much distance. Patients have a wide range of reactions to the therapist's expression of emotion, including concerns about the therapist's vulnerability and resilience. But the patient will also be moved that they could have such a powerful impact on them.

Warren Poland (2020) highlights that the therapist's vulnerability is an essential aspect of working psychoanalytically with patients. "My sense of pleasure when starting any psychoanalytic venture with someone new is always touched by a tinge of fear, my awareness that wherever the new work goes will be bound to include areas where I myself do not want to go, and that whatever will come up to trouble and frighten me will never be what I might predict at the start." Expecting and, paradoxically, hoping to be deeply and uncomfortably impacted by the patient contributes to developing a psychoanalytic process that provides the best opportunity for meaningful change.

A therapist tries to maintain a consistent sense of safety in the consulting room, knowing that, without it, no psychotherapy will be productive. In every psychotherapeutic session, the therapist also tries to understand the ways in which the patient does not feel secure, where their hesitation, tone of voice, change of subject, slip of the tongue, or other "action" points toward the leading edge of vulnerability. Given the personal vulnerabilities which every therapist possesses, productive psychotherapy requires that the therapist feel "safe" within themselves. A sense of safety within oneself allows those times when one is moved to tears, frustration, or exasperation to be moments of deep intimacy, not filled with shame and embarrassment.

Feeling "safe enough" within oneself makes it less likely that treatment will be harmfully shaped by both the patient's and the therapist's unconscious determination to avoid certain intensities developing between them. Feeling safe enough within oneself allows therapists to respect and welcome those moments when they lose their psychoanalytic balance.

◇◇

GIFTS.

"Merry Christmas," says Mr. F., handing me the wrapped box he had concealed under his coat and quickly closing the door as he leaves, surprising me on the first holiday season we have shared. All the more surprising was unwrapping the present to find a wine I knew to be extremely expensive. The cost of the wine was no problem for Mr. F.; money was not the issue. The question was whether the therapy would be better served by accepting the gift or by returning it. An exploration of what he was communicating with the gift would accompany either choice.

In my opinion, the standard of never accepting a gift from any patient at any time and always deciding only to explore its meaning spares the therapist from the uncomfortable position of wrestling with the decision each time. The response to the offer of a gift is, from this perspective, similar to the response to missed psychotherapeutic sessions. Which will better further the treatment: acceptance or refusal? With regard to Mr. F.'s powerfully tempting gift (I love good wine), I decided the better choice was to turn it down. The better choice? Although we were able to explore how uncomfortable he was expressing his deep, genuine gratitude, had I accepted the wine we might have had a different but meaningful conversation about its meaning.

PATIENTS WHO COME TO THE OFFICE WHEN LIKELY CONTAGIOUS.

Mr. G., whose mother died when he was three, had deeply unsettling reactions to any missed session and could be counted on to make Herculean efforts to attend every one. One morning, after arranging himself comfortably in the chair, he sneezed loudly, rushing to grab a tissue. "I have a cold," he said, "but I feel well enough to be here. I don't think I am contagious, and I did not want to miss this session, especially since you will be away for the next two weeks."

I wondered whether Mr. G. wished to infect me for abandoning him for two weeks, but he and I had just begun to explore how he managed his aggression, and he seemed nowhere near ready to consider that possibility now. I was faced with the dilemma of whether I was willing to run the risk of catching his cold. Although I knew he would have a strong reaction that couldn't be fully explored until my return, I told him that while I understood the importance of this session, I did not want to risk getting sick, especially since I was about to go on vacation, and that we would have to end our session. As a rule, we do our patients no favors by letting them put us at risk or by not cancelling an appointment due to our own illness.

ENDING

Like most therapists, I establish definite times for my meetings with patients; we both know when they will begin and when they will end. Often we have believed that continuing our conversation would be helpful and we have regretted its ending. Sometimes both of us have been relieved to know that a tortured, challenging dialogue would end at the scheduled time, and occasionally a patient has concluded an intense, unsettling session by leaving before the time was up. Jacques Lacan, a French psychoanalyst, preferred to have "variable" sessions in which the length of each conversation with a patient would be shaped by the nature of the conversation. Ending this book at this point seems very Lacanian. It just feels like the right time to stop.

◇◇◇◇◇◇◇◇◇◇◇◇◇◇◇◇◇◇◇◇◇◇◇◇◇◇◇◇◇◇◇◇◇◇◇◇◇◇◇

WHEN DECIDING HOW LONG TO PRACTICE, BE SURE THE PATIENT IS THE PRIMARY BENEFICIARY OF YOUR DECISION.

Several years before I began this project, I reached the difficult decision to end my clinical practice shortly before my 82nd birthday. Ironically, creating the ending of this book coincided with the end of my clinical practice. I have continued teaching, supervising, consulting, and being active within my psychoanalytic institute. I have no intention of retiring my psychoanalytic mind.

Deciding when to end a piece of writing, like deciding when to end a psychotherapeutic relationship, or when to close one's clinical career, is arbitrary. There is always more that seems worthy of inclusion, just as there are always further gains to be accomplished clinically. Both decisions seemed very right, and I have had no second thoughts. But I know that my reactions to closing my clinical practice shaped, in ways I cannot quite express, the tenor of drawing this piece of writing to a close.

I decided not to title this section "Conclusion," a word that, to me, suggests a more final closure. Writing is a dialogue with imagined readers, and even though I will not be participating with your reactions to my book, I hope that reading my words will have involved you in an active dialogue with me. When a patient and I decide to stop working together, I do not conceptualize it as a termination but rather as an ending of our regularly scheduled conversations. The process that we have created over the years of speaking and working together will not end; only our regular time together and our psychoanalytic conversations will end.

If the experiences of my patients are anything like mine, they will often review these conversations and our relationship and will see me and themselves from new perspectives. I hope there will be many instances when they wish that we could resume our conversations. So with ending my manuscript. What follows is not a conclusion, but rather an end to my "dialogue" with you, a dialogue that I hope has been meaningful, thought-provoking and, like a productive psychoanalysis, will continue to stimulate your thinking.

As I struggled with the challenges of retirement, I discovered *The Empty Couch* (2013), a collection of essays by experienced, respected psychoanalysts from many countries. The essays explored the broad topic of the analyst's aging, the impact of age upon their practice, illness in the analyst, and the intense struggles that most wage about retirement. The broad-reaching and thought-provoking essays helped to clarify further how and when I wanted to stop my clinical work, but I found many of the chapters overly theoretical and philosophical, focusing on the analyst's omnipotence, grandiosity, and denial of death. While these contributions were focused and thought-provoking, the more personal contributions were meaningful in a very different way.

By the time I began to write the ending of this book, I realized that I wanted to be very explicit about how I organized my retirement. I also want to emphasize strongly that this is what has worked well for me. Every analyst needs to create their own, very personal ending to their practice, much as they created their own very personal manner of practicing.

I decided that I would end my clinical work before I reached my 82nd birthday. I did not want to end my practice too close to my birthday. Retirement was not a cause for celebration. I did not want to end my practice near a significant holiday or near my annual August vacation, and so I selected the end of February 2023, six weeks before my 82nd birthday. I made this decision several years earlier. I was and remain in good health, and believed that my psychoanalytic work was more thoughtful, better attuned, and more productive than it had ever been. Far from feeling burned out, I continued to find my work satisfying and meaningful.

My decision to retire at 82 was determined by my having seen, firsthand, the profound and sometimes tragic consequences that a clinician's illness or sudden death can have on patients. For many years, I was a member of the Impaired Physicians Committee of the District of Columbia Medical Society. As an analyst, I served as a member and later chaired the Colleague Assistance Committee of my psychoanalytic center. I personally knew too many respected psychoanalytic friends and colleagues who continued to practice despite being impaired by substance abuse, serious illness, or by the inexorable waning of their cognitive abilities. And, there were those colleagues for whom sudden death took the decision about whether to continue their practice out of their hands (Galatzer-Levy 2004). Quite simply, I was not willing to gamble past the age of 82.

My desire not to injure my patients or sully my professional integrity overrode my imagined omnipotence, denial of death, and desire to continue immersing myself in work I found so fulfilling. At 80, my friend and mentor, Earle Silber, ended both his clinical practice and all his activities as a teacher and supervisor. Although I was not aware of it, even though we had taught a class together, he knew that his memory was beginning to deteriorate. I admired his courage to leave the profession he loved and, when he later developed severe dementia, I was grateful that neither he nor his patients had to endure its impact on their work. I subsequently came to believe that continuing to practice until one is no longer able to do so or dies is profoundly unethical.

I wrestled with how much notice I should give to my patients, and, in discussions with colleagues, got a range of responses and recommendations. Although I did not inform patients at that time, I selected a definite date to stop several years prior to my retirement. That decision profoundly changed my state of mind. Although it was rarely conscious, I am certain every session was, to some degree, shaped by my knowledge that the patient and I had limited time to work together. How that knowledge was woven into the fabric of my work, I do not know, but I am certain that I must have subtly tried to accelerate the pace of treatment. No patient gave any indication of being aware of the change, but I remain convinced that I was bringing the ball past midcourt more quickly, saving precious psychoanalytic seconds.

I decided to inform patients one year before my retirement, but well before then, a number of patients asked how long I planned to practice. After some exploration of the question, I chose to answer, but I also said that, had they not asked, I would have told them one year prior to the date of my retirement. I also said that I had not told my other patients; I very much did not want anyone to be injured by learning of my decision through the grapevine.

Many colleagues thought that a year's notice was much too long. One friend thought that I would be subjecting myself to a year of torture and wondered why I wanted to do that to myself.

For a number of reasons, including my own early experiences with endings, a year remained a comfortable period for me. Although I had wanted to inform all my patients during the same week, some were in a deeply unsettled place, and I postponed informing them until they had regained their psychological equilibrium. I also decided that I would continue working with several patients who were 90 or older. To ask them to develop a relationship with a new therapist at this point in their lives seemed much too burdensome. In addition, I also did not think it unethical to gamble that I would remain healthy and fully competent for the rest of their lives.

Ending my practice in this way had two benefits, neither of which I had considered. One was that my office colleagues were spared the very possible burden of calling all of my patients to inform them of my death or serious illness and to arrange for any care they might need. The second benefit was that I was able to postpone the end of treatment for several patients who encountered very stressful events only weeks before the last day we were to meet. I also strongly urged all patients who had moved from Washington and continued to speak with me by phone to come to Washington for our final meeting. Almost all made the effort and found it very meaningful.

I ended with nearly everyone during the same week. Since I could not identify any criteria to use in deciding who should end sooner, I chose simply to have the final week's schedule remain unchanged, but I am certain that some patients paid the price of my having to metabolize all my endings in the same week. I know I was not at the top of my game. In retrospect, I would have drawn lots and had 25% of my patients end during a given week of my last month. That would, of course, have "shortchanged" 75% of my patients, but should they have focused on that, I would have understood their unhappiness as deflecting attention away from the ending and wondered whether it was a final burst of sibling rivalry. As was true in all my professional work, as I organized the specifics of my retirement, I did not treat those patients I saw once per week any differently from those I saw 4-5 times per week.

I recommended that patients wait a number of months before beginning work with someone else, but I also assured them that, if, at any time, they wished to begin treatment, I would facilitate a referral. I believed that this period would allow patients to experience fully their reactions to ending our work together, to gain some perspective on their analysis, to experience life without analysis, and to clarify what they hoped to accomplish should they begin treatment with someone else. The months without a therapeutic relationship also buffered the temptation to shroud their reactions to the end of therapy by replacing one analyst with another, as if that were in any way possible.

In the months after my patients were informed of my retirement, I often had to sit, as comfortably as possible, with the feelings of being an abandoning, self-centered mother/father whose retirement could easily have been delayed. Although profoundly uncomfortable, that reaction came as no surprise. I was, however, caught completely off guard by the awareness that I had conceptualized my work as attempting to provide good psychoanalytic mothering and good psychoanalytic fathering. I had tried to create a nurturing, growth-promoting experience by developing a totally unique relationship and interpersonal environment, built upon the foundation of my person, education, and experience. These aspects of myself became the nucleus of each psychoanalytic cell.

I was naive and arrogant enough to believe that I was fully pre-pared to metabolize and absorb my sorrow at no longer facilitating and sharing the transformations and journeys of my patients. I imagined I would readily digest the disappointment of having no future psychoanalytic journeys of this kind. But I was astoundingly unprepared for my response to voluntarily surrendering the experience of psychoanalytic parenting, a process so evocative of my experience fathering my own children. I was knocked off balance not so much by the sorrow and regret that I deprived my patients of a natural end to our work together, but by my awareness that nothing could replace the myriad, undefinable ways in which my relationship with each patient transformed me, nourishing my self in a manner that was as unique as the analytic work itself.

The process and the privilege of developing a deep psycho-analytic relationship, both personal and professional, facilitated my own transformations, not as dramatic as those achieved by my patients, but most definitely pervasive and deeply meaningful. I felt like a child who runs away from home and yet feels they have been abandoned by their parents. I felt that psychoanalysis had abandoned me, leaving me hurt, bewildered, and frightened.

I have come to understand that, for me, the practice of psycho-analysis had become what I conceptualize as an "experiential object," a deeply meaningful aspect of one's life that has unconsciously been infused with a range of thoughts and emotions. My relationship with psychoanalysis, like each psychoanalyst's relationship with their profession, was as unique as each child's relationship with a transitional object. Like a relationship with other objects, until the loss has actually occurred, one cannot imagine or understand its profound impact.

If my experience is not unique, it seems likely that one of the many factors contributing to an analyst's reluctance to retire is the unconscious avoidance of losing the enriching nourishment that one gains from this special object relationship with the profession of psychoanalysis. Retirement from clinical work has not created concern about whether I will live productively and meaningfully in my remaining years, but I am painfully aware that nothing can replace the stimulation and nourishment that my clinical career has provided.

I hope that my riffs on these aphorisms have allowed you to get some sense of my personal, "analytic attitude" (Schafer 1983). Schafer's attitude toward his patients and the profession of psychoanalysis conveyed a remarkable ability to think critically and re-evaluate the foundational beliefs of the field of psychoanalysis. His constantly evolving theoretical beliefs and his understanding of patients always implied that we should be wary of believing that we "understand" our patients. I hope that the spirit of open inquiry that was so central to his life's work has been reflected in the thoughts I have collected.

I was certain that writing this book would take me on any number of unexpected byways. In its own unique way, writing, like associating freely, is a subtly altered state of consciousness, a dialogue with the less conscious aspects of oneself. By the time I was nearing the completion of this book, I had come to realize that my person was even more central to my ability or inability to help my patients than I had believed. I also realized that the persons of my two very different analysts had had an even more pervasive impact on me than I'd appreciated.

At the end of my freshman year of college, Brand Blanshard, a renowned philosopher, was giving the last lecture of his career. He was a gifted speaker, and his final talk had such a powerful impact that it came to mind as I was writing this ending. This soft-spoken, compelling man ended his career by sharing with us, students who were just beginning to conceive of ours, words allegedly spoken by Socrates at his trial: "The unexamined life is not worth living."

As I neared the ending of this book and my clinical work, I understood much more deeply the profound impact of examining one's life and how central that process is to creating meaning. Creating and living the life of a psychoanalyst has been a privilege. That life included coming to know my patients in the deepest way and assisting them to live more comfortably within themselves—ironically, more comfortably precisely because they had been able to discover so many hidden, often painful, aspects of themselves. Living my life as a psychoanalyst has nurtured many transformations and allowed me to become more at home within myself. For that I will be forever grateful.

ACKNOWLEDGMENTS

I chose to close this endeavor with my acknowledgments, knowing full well that they are often put at the beginning of a manuscript. By ending with acknowledgments, I want to emphasize how profoundly my development as a person, physician, psychiatrist, and psycho-analyst has been nurtured, stimulated, guided, and encouraged by the relationships I have been fortunate to have. Martha Adler, Yvonne Decuir, Ellen Luria, Aimee Nover, and Bob Nover read an earlier draft of this book. Their careful reading and thoughtful suggestions sharpened my focus. Dick Fritsch also read an earlier manuscript, generously offering specific reactions and suggestions with sticky notes attached to many pages. My friend and colleague, Marc Levine, a remarkable photographer as well as psychoanalyst, took the photograph of my office which is on the cover of this book.

My students challenged me to clarify and re-examine my pre-conceptions and convictions and reinforced the necessity to explain psychoanalytic concepts clearly and succinctly. To my patients, I cannot adequately express my gratitude for the privilege of working with and learning so much from you. Your contributions are on every page. I very much hope that the person who comes alive in this book resembles the person you got to know in my consulting room. The team at Mission Point Press were most supportive and made many thoughtful suggestions. Hart Cauchy, the editor from

Mission Point Press, thoughtfully, patiently, and carefully edited my manuscript, patiently enduring my revisions, and making certain that my words were readily understandable.

Most importantly, I want to acknowledge, as best I can, the innumerable ways in which my wife of 60 years has supported, stimulated, and contributed to my personal and professional growth. Alice has reviewed and edited everything I have written and every talk I have given, always providing thoughtful, informed contributions, not always easy to receive, but always spot on. Were it not for her steadfast confidence in the meaningfulness of what I wanted to convey, my doubts and reservations might well have led me to abandon this endeavor. Words could never be enough to express my gratitude and deep admiration. These words most certainly are not.

BIBLIOGRAPHY

Allen, J.G., Fonagy, P. and Bateman, A.W. (2008). *Mentalizing in Clinical Practice*. American Psychiatric Publishing, VA.

Arlow, J. (1995). Stilted Listening: Psychoanalysis as Discourse. *Psychoanalytic Quarterly*, 64: 215–233.

Barthes, R. (1991). *The Responsibility of Forms: Critical Essays on Music, Art, and Representation*. University of California Press, Berkeley and Los Angeles.

Beebe, B. and Lachman, F. (2002). Organizing Principles of Interaction from Infant Research and the Prediction of Lifespan Attachment. *J. Infant, Child, Adolescent Psychotherapy*, 2: 61–89.

Benveniste, D.S. (2021). Mother-Infant Observations: A View into the Wordless Social Instincts that form the Foundation of Human Psychodynamics. *J. American Psychoanalytic Assoc.*, 69: 33–50.

Bion, W. (1967). Notes on Memory and Desire. In Wilfred Bion, *Los Angeles Seminars and Supervision*. ed. J. Jaguayo and B. Malin, London, Karnac, 136–8.

Brenner, C. (1979). Working Alliance, Therapeutic Alliance, and Transference. *J. American Psychoanalytic Assoc.*, 27: 137–157.

Busch, F. (2006). Countertransference in Defense Enactments. *J. American Psychoanalytic Assoc.*, 54: 67–85.

Carlat, D. J. (2010). *Unhinged: The Trouble with Psychiatry: A Doctor's Revelations about a Profession in Crisis*. Free Press, New York.

Chused, J. F. (1988). The Role of Enactments. *Psychoanalytic Dialogues*, 13: 677–87.

Chused, J.F. (1988). The Transference Neurosis in Child Analysis. *Psychoanalytic Study of the Child*, 43: 51-81.

Diagnostic and Statistical Manual of Mental Disorders, 5th edition. (2013). American Psychiatric Publishing, Washington, DC.

First, M. B. (2005). Clinical utility: A prerequisite for the adoption of a dimensional approach in DSM. *J. of Abnormal Psychology*, 114: 560-64.

Frances, A. (2013). *Saving Normal: An Insider's Revolt Against Out-of-control Psychiatric Diagnosis, DSM V, Big Pharma, and the Medicalization of Ordinary Life*. Harper Collins, NY.

Freud, S. (1905). *A Fragment of a Case of Hysteria*. Std. Edition, 7: 1–122, London.

Freud, S. (1912). *Recommendations to Physicians Practising Psychoanalysis*. Std. Edition. 12: 109–120, London.

Freud, S. (1916). *Some Character Types Met within Psycho-analytic Work*. Std. Edition 14: 309–333, London.

Gabbard, G.O. (2022). The Decline and Fall of Neutrality in Psychoanalytic Discourse. *J. American Psychoanalytic Assoc.*, 70: 309–315.

Galatzer-Levy, R.M. (2004). The Death of the Analyst. *J. American Psychoanalytic Assoc.*, 52: 999–1024.

Gill, M. (1979). The Analysis of the Transference. *J. American Psychoanalytic Assoc.*, 27: 263–288.

Gornick, V. (1998). In: *Living to Tell the Tale*, J.T. McDonnell. Penguin Books.

Greenberg, G. (2013). *The Book of Woe: The DSM and the Unmaking of Psychiatry*. Blue Rider Press, New York.

Greenson, R. (1965). The Working Alliance and the Transference Neurosis. *Psychoanalytic Quarterly*, 34: 155–181.

Hart, A. (2022). Discussion of Gabbard, Holmes, and Portuges. *J. American Psychoanalytic Assoc.*, 70: 335–49.

Holmes, D.E. (2022). Neutrality is not Neutral. *J. American Psychoanalytic Assoc.*, 70: 317–22.

Horwitz, A. V. (2021). *DSM: A History of Psychiatry's Bible*. Johns Hopkins Press, Baltimore, MD.

Isaacson, W. (2011). *Steve Jobs*. Simon and Schuster, New York.

Joseph, D. I. (1990). The Fundamental Rule: Its Utilization in the Conversion of Psychoanalytic Psychotherapy to Psychoanalysis. *Psychoanalytic Inquiry*, 10: 88–106.

Junkers, G., Ed. (2013). *The Empty Couch*. Routledge, New York.

Kanwal, G. (2023). Integrative Individuation: An Alternative to the Separation-Individuation Model. *J. American Psychoanalytic Assoc.*, 71: 419–444.

Kleinman, A. (1988, 2020). *The Illness Narratives: Suffering, Healing and the Human Condition*. Basic Books, New York.

Kleinman, A. (1988). *Rethinking Psychiatry: From Cultural Category to Personal Experience*. Free Press, New York.

Lakoff, G. and Johnson, M.V. (1999). *Philosophy in the Flesh: The Embodied Mind and its Challenge to Western Thought*. Basic Books, New York.

Langs, R. (1978). Validation and the Framework of the Therapeutic Situation-Thoughts Prompted by Hans H. Strupp's "Suffering and Psychotherapy." *Contemporary Psychoanalysis*, 14: 98–124.

Lear, J. (2004). *Therapeutic Action, An Earnest Plea for Irony*. Other Press, New York.

Loewald, H. (1960). On the Therapeutic Action of Psycho-Analysis. *Int. J. Psychoanalysis*, 41: 16–33.

Mahler, M., Pine, F., and Bergman, A. (1975). *The Psychological Birth of the Human Infant*. Basic Books, New York.

Malcolm, J. (1981). *Psychoanalysis: The Impossible Profession*. Vintage Books, New York.

Mark, T. L., Levit, K.R. and Buck, J.A. (2009). Datapoints: Psychotropic Drug Prescriptions by Medical Specialty. *Psychiatric Services*, 60: 9.

McDonnell, J. T. (1998). *Living to Tell the Tale*. Penguin Books, New York.

Moerman, D. (2002). *Meaning, Medicine and the Placebo Effect*. Cambridge University Press, Cambridge, UK.

Ogden, T. (1992). *The Primitive Edge of Experience*. Rowman and Littlefield, New York.

Ogden, T. (1992). Transference and Countertransference in the Initial Analytic Meeting. *Psychoanalytic Inquiry*, 12: 225–247.

Pine, F. (2011). Beyond Pluralism: Psychoanalysis and the Workings of Mind. *Psychoanalytic Quarterly*, 80: 823-856.

Poland, W. S. (1975). Tact as a Psychoanalytic Function. *International J. of Psychoanalysis*, 56: 155–62.

Poland, W. S. (1992). Transference: "An Original Creation." *Psychoanalytic Quarterly*, 61: 185-205.

Poland, W. S. (2000). The Analyst's Witnessing and Otherness. *International J. of Psychoanalysis*, 48: 17–34.

Poland, W. S. (2018). *Intimacy and Separateness in Psychoanalysis*. Routledge, New York.

Portuges, S.H. (2022). Neutrality as a White Lie: Psychoanalytic Neutrality, Race and Racism. *J. American Psychoanalytic Assoc.*, 70: 323–334.

Quinodoz, J-M (1993). *The Taming of Solitude: Separation Anxiety in Psychoanalysis*. Routledge, London.

Rako, S. and Mazer, H. (1980). *Semrad: The Heart of a Therapist*. J. Aronson, Lanham, Maryland.

Reiser, M. (1988). Are Psychiatric Educators "Losing the Mind"? *American J. Psychiatry*, 145: 148–53.

Schafer, R. (1976). *A New Language for Psychoanalysis*. Yale Univ. Press, New Haven, CT.

Schafer, R. (1983). *The Analytic Attitude*. Basic Books, New York.

Schafer, R. (1992). *Retelling a Life: Narration and Dialogue in Psychoanalysis*. Basic Books, New York.

Schafer, R. (1999). Disappointment and Disappointedness. *International J. of Psychoanalysis*, 80: 1093–1104.

Spiro, H. M. (1986). *Doctors, Patients, and Placebos*. Yale University Press, New Haven, CT.

Stern, D. B. (1983). Unformulated Experience: From Familiar Chaos to Creative Disorder. *Contemp. Psychoanalysis*, 19: 71–99.

Stern, D. B. (2023). Distance and Relation: Emerging from Embeddedness in the Other. *J. American Psychoanalytic Assoc.*, 71: 641–668.

Sullivan, H. S. (1953). *The Interpersonal Theory of Psychiatry*. Norton, New York.

Szasz, Thomas (1961). *The Myth of Mental Illness*. Secker and Warburg, New York.

Wachtel, P. L. (1977). *Psychoanalysis and Behavior Therapy: Toward an Integration*. Basic Books, New York.

Wordsworth, William. *The Excursion*. Longman, Hurst, Rees, Orme, and Brown, 1820, 191–192.

Yeats, W. B. "Among School Children." *The Collected Poems of W. B. Yeats*. Simon and Schuster, 1989, New York, 219.

Zetzel, E. (1970). The Therapeutic Alliance in the Analysis of Hysteria. In *The Capacity for Emotional Growth*, 182–196.

INDEX

AUTHOR INDEX

ABOUT THE AUTHOR

David Joseph has practiced psychiatry and psychoanalysis for over fifty years. In addition to his private practice, he has served as the director of residency training at St. Elizabeths Hospital in Washington, DC. He is an active member of the Washington Baltimore Center for Psychoanalysis where he is a training and supervising analyst and has served as president of the board and chair of the Institute Council. He is a clinical professor at The George Washington University Department of Psychiatry and Behavioral Sciences.

David and his wife, Alice, are avid collectors of American folk art. They reside in an eighteenth-century farmhouse in Chevy Chase, Maryland, with their quizzical sheepadoodle, Arlo.

www.ingramcontent.com/pod-product-compliance
Lightning Source LLC
Chambersburg PA
CBHW022048020426
42335CB00012B/602